R. Buckminster Fuller

An Autobiographical Monologue/Scenario

Buckminster Fuller

utobiographical Monologue/Scenario

Documented and Edited by
Robert Snyder

T. MARTIN'S PRESS, NEW YORK

Acknowledgements

My gratitude to my "picture-book team," editor, Ruth Glushanok and designer, Kadi Karist Tint, who resisted my excessive selection of word and picture from the miles of film and tape I'd recorded, in compliance with the very essence of my mercurial subject: to do more with less, evermore with everless.

My gratitude to our brilliant editor at St. Martin's, Michael Denneny, whose creative insight changed our direction from an informal overview to an autobiographical portrait, and to his assistant, Paul Dinas, who helped us make this difficult transition.

My gratitude to the cinematographers, who from 1951 to the present recorded Bucky and his work: Kent Wakeford, Kenneth Snelson, Bayliss Glascock, Gary Conklin, Martin Andrews III; to Einar Moos and John Ferry (of my staff at Masters & Masterworks Productions) for preparation of the stills from the film frames; to Medard Gabel, Timothy Wessels and Peter Kent (of Bucky's staff) for selection of stills and text from Bucky's archives; to stills photographers: Hans Wild (cover photo), M.A.C. Miles (production stills at Bear Island); Wernher Krutein, Hugh Kenner, Claude Johnston (portraits); Alexandre Georges; Jay Maisel; Syeus Mottel; Don Richter; Sam Rosenberg; and John Warren ("events photos"—domes and such); other sources: A.P., the Bettman Archive, Cal Tech, Division of Records and Archives State of North Carolina, Hale Observatories, Kraushaar Gallery, Time Inc., UPI. And my sincere apologies to the sources we could not trace.

SNYDER, ROBERT.
BUCKMINSTER FULLER:
AN AUTOBIOGRAPHICAL MONOLOGUE/SCENARIO
1. *FULLER*, RICHARD BUCKMINSTER, 1895-
2. ENGINEERS—UNITED STATES—BIOGRAPHY. 3. ARCHITECTS
—UNITED STATES—BIOGRAPHY. I. TITLE.
A140.F9S64   620'.0092'4 [B]   79-16323

ISBN 0-312-10678-5

PREFACE

Being neither scientist nor philosopher, I cannot even attempt to explain Buckminster Fuller. Bucky's own writings do that; notably, his life-work, *Synergetics: Explorations in the Geometry of Thinking*, volumes I and II. One of his great virtues as a teacher is that he never patronizes his audience, young or old, since he assumes that if he, the self-styled "low-average man" can understand anything abstract or concrete—for him only two facets of the same phenomenon—so can anyone. Then, too, there is a constant proliferation of his inventions, his artifacts, which are elegant demonstrations of the generalized principles he has drawn from his close study of the cosmos. For this layman, his Expo dome is "pure principle made visible."

For those who need or want critical evaluation, there are a few splendid books by E.J. Applewhite, Hugh Kenner, John McHale, William Marlin; "popular" pieces such as: *Time's* cover story; *Life's* portrait by Barry Ferrell; and the *New Yorker* profile by Calvin Tomkins. A handbook of both ideas and inventions is readily available in Robert Marks and Fuller's *The Dymaxion World of Buckminster Fuller.*

For that matter, there are my films: the ten-minute vignette in "Sketchbook No.1: Three Americans"; the half-hour "Introduction to the World Game"; the half-hour "Primer of the Universe"; the one-hour television special "Buckminster Fuller on Spaceship Earth"; the eighty-five minute expansion thereof, "The World of Buckminster Fuller"; and most recently, the one-hour television special, "Reflections: Buckminster Fuller." They're getting around more and more, here and around the world.

Since they were all done on a one-to-one basis—"from the horse's mouth"—they are the principal sources for this book. But, while one critic wrote of *The World of Buckminster Fuller*, "As pure a record of Buckminster Fuller as would be possible to make... his is the only voice we hear; indeed his voice and *persona* are the film.... This is the definitive record of one of the great teachers of our time transcribed in sight and sound for the archives of posterity,"—they still did not capture enough of the human being behind the public figure of a "protean genius," the "Leonardo da Vinci of our time."

Wouldn't it be wonderful if everyone could encounter him, as our family has at Christmastime, when Bucky plays Santa Claus to the hilt; or summertime at his spiritual home-retreat on Bear Island, where he rows and sails; tells funny stories; composes doggerel poems; sings (in an off-key, monotone croaking) turn-of-the-century ballads and sea shanties; tells impish jokes and dances Irish jigs or the be-bop. Here, too, his most fundamental characteristics become apparent: the boy scout in the wonderland of nature; so curious, through his tri-focal lenses, about everything visible—macrocosm, microcosm, and the mesocosm, man in between all at once—and exploring the mysteries of the invisible; making "trial balances," not only those of his inventive artifacts, but also of his hypothetical generalized pinciples.

If a book can't directly convey all of this, then the next best thing, our editor suggested, would be for me—from my privileged vantage point of an intimate personal and working relationship with Bucky over more than thirty years—to offer some intimate glimpses of the human being; and since, as we shall see, the man, his ideas and his work are a deliberate self-creation, a work of art, then my selections from our hours of film and tape should be in the form of an autobiographical monologue/scenario (copiously illustrated). As we follow this self-creation, it will become clear that he is a marvelous composite of Yankee pragmatism (the inventions) and more importantly, of the deep streak of New England Transcendentalism (the ideas, the generalized principles, which he claims bring us closest to Nature-God). I would venture to say that Emerson's essay "Self-Reliance" is his bible, especially the last sentence: "Whoso would be a man, must be a nonconformist." Bucky's been that from his earliest years, and, I daresay, will be that forever.

This book is dedicated to my beloved son, Jaime L. Snyder (Bucky's equally beloved grandson) and all his fellow passengers on spaceship earth—those "into" Bucky and those who should be—in the hope that they won't ever be discouraged by the "slings and arrows of outrageous fortune," but rather find inspiration from Bucky's resounding life-yea-saying why-nots.

1895–1927:
FROM BIRTH TO REBIRTH

Imagine yourselves in terms of a moving-picture scenario...

You've all seen moving pictures
run backwards,
where people undive out of
the swimming pool back onto the board.
I'm going to
run a moving picture of you backwards.
You've just had breakfast;
now, I'm going to run the picture backward
and all the food comes out of your mouth
onto the plate;
and the plates go back
up onto the serving tray
and things go back
into the stove, back into the icebox;
they come out of the icebox
and into the cans,
and they go back to the store;
and then, from the store
they go back to the wholesalesaler;
then they go back to the
factories where they've been put together;
then they go back to the trucks and ships;
and they finally get back to pineapples
in Hawaii.

Then the pineapples separate out,
go back into the air;
the raindrops go back into the sky,
and so forth.
But in the very fast accelerated reversal
of a month
practically everything has come together
that you now have on board you,
gradually becoming your hair and your skin
and so forth,
whereas a month ago,
it was some air coming over the mountains.
In other words, you get completely deployed.
I want you to begin to think of yourselves
in an interesting way
as each one of these.

If we had some way
of putting tracers on the pictures,
you would see chemical elements
gradually getting closer and closer
together, and, finally, getting into those
various vegetable places and into roasts
and, tighter and tighter, into cans,
into the store,
finally getting to just being you or me—
temporarily, becoming my hair, my ear,
some part of my skin—
and then that breaks up and goes off
and gets blown around as dust.

Each of us is a very complex pattern
integrity with which we were born.

I was born cross-eyed, almost blind.

My eyes are very misshapen, so I am very farsighted.
As a child I didn't know there was anything wrong with me. I assumed everybody else saw as I did. I couldn't see any details; I just saw colors. My mother couldn't understand why I was continually falling in love with a different shade of green or purple.

In my early childhood I learned to rely on my sense of smell because I couldn't see details, such as people's eyes, and so I began to know people and their personalities by how they smelled.

I knew the smell of everyone in the house. That's how I could tell whether I was going to like someone or not. The people that didn't smell right to me never did work out.

From the family album —

At four and a half they took me to an eye doctor who gave me corrective lenses. Imagine my surprise when I got my glasses for the first time and could see human eyes, cat's eyes, and the eyes of snakes!

Everybody seemed to be communicating through their eyes. I hadn't had that kind of communication before, the communication of feelings of love and warmth that people around me felt.

If I had to find one word that would describe the phenomenon of life—the experience of life—it would be the word awareness. The very consequence of awareness is to impose the phenomenon time upon an eternal universe.

When there is no otherness, there is no awareness. So it was otherness I was first aware of, and the otherness was the motherliness of hands on me, the source of warmth, and food coming in.

With mother, father, Leslie

After glasses: With cousins and Uncle Waldo

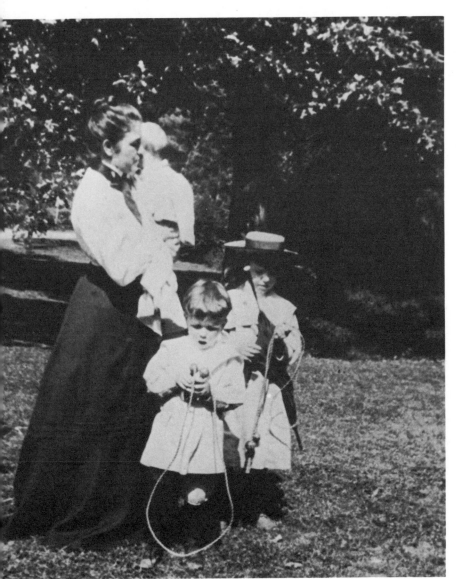

With mother, Leslie, and baby Rosy

One of the most interesting things in my life is that while opticians kept giving me increased magnification as I got older, I still have the same correction, so all I have to do is take off my glasses to see what I saw when I was four and a half.

When I take them off I can't see any human eyes.
I see shadowy areas on
the face and the color of the face and the color of the hair, but no really sharp lines.

One of my first days at kindergarten the teacher brought us some toothpicks and semi-dried peas and told us to make structures.

The other children, who had good eyes, were familiar with houses and barns; with my bad sight, I was used to seeing only bulks—I had no feeling at all about structural lines.

Because I couldn't see, I naturally had recourse to my other senses which were very sensitive. When the teacher told me to make structures, I tried to make something that would work.

Pushing and pulling, I found that a triangle held its shape when nothing else did. The other children made rectangular structures that seemed to stand up because the peas held them in shape. Meanwhile, after pushing and pulling, the triangle I made felt good.

The teacher called all the other teachers in the primary school as well as the kindergarten, to look at this triangular structure. I remember being surprised that they were surprised.

I began to feel then that all nature's structuring and patterning must be based on triangles.

All through my first years, my sister Leslie, who was three years older, had been telling me all the things she could see. Children have tremendous imaginations and I thought she was making it all up like the fairy stories she read me, so that I would be inventive too and tell her all the things I could see.

I was always getting a laugh so I thought I was doing great. It made me very happy to have people laugh at my stories. Then when I got my glasses I realized my sister hadn't been telling me stories at all. This really became a dilemma because now people were expecting me to do some imaginative thing to entertain them and kept encouraging me to do it.

From this point on I would be a little liar. I found people like a lie, and I could invent any kind of experience I wanted to—which was really too bad. My mother was the most lovely mother, but people kept persuading her that she must be very stern with this little child. So I was continually getting spankings and, nine times out of ten, I didn't know why I was being spanked. I was doing what a child is intended to do—using my imagination. So to avoid what seemed to be leading up to a spanking, I would use my imagination and story-telling ability to misinform my mother. This has built a trait into me which I've had to cope with as the years went on.

There were four of us children—Leslie was the oldest, then I, Wolcott, and Rosie was the baby. We lived in a rather large Gay Nineties Victorian house in Milton, outside of Boston, on about two and a half acres with woods, and when I was young my mother had plenty of help, my sister and I each had a nurse, there was a gardener and a cook. When my father got sick all of them disappeared except the cook, who had an enormous influence on my life.

I was twelve years old when my father gave me a real tiny bike
and I remember the experience of going faster than with my legs, and goin
through the driveway and through the beautiful apple orchards.
How beautiful spring was on a bicycle.
My father and mother each had a bicycle and we would go off early in
the morning.
Those early mornings…
I particularly loved coming down to absolute silence in the house;
everything seemed so peaceful and nature was waking up.
I loved to be there at dawn on a beautiful snowy day after it had been
snowing all night,
and go out around our place. There were little tracks of birds
and wonderful first motions of life all around.

I really loved coming home.
Whenever I went off skating or going to school—
and I enjoyed all those things tremendously—
I really loved coming home and my mother would have hot tea waiting.
I tend to remember the winters almost more than spring.

So I was really shocked at the difference between my life at home and wha
my grandmother told me about the golden rule—that life is meant to be
loving, peaceful, thoughtful to one another—and being faced with the
reality when I got out into the world to find things rough.

Posing with my bicycle in front of school

Our house in Milton

My father became a merchant rather than going into banking or stocks, and
being a merchant seemed to agree with him. Boston was a great shoe-
manufacturing town; the first mass producer of shoes in America. And my
father imported leathers from Argentina and India for the shoe trade. He
brought us into another social world. Father was an exception in our family

The Fuller side of my family was well-known for its long line of intellectual
and rebels—Unitarian ministers, lawyers, writers—from my great-grandfather, the Reverend Timothy Fuller, who was a delegate from Massachusett
to the Constituent Assembly but opposed the ratification of the Constitution
because it didn't prohibit slavery; and Timothy Jr., who graduated second
instead of first in the Harvard class of 1801 because he took part in a
student rebellion; to my grandfather, an all-out abolitionist, who was killed
leading a successful Union attack at Fredericksburg.

Unitarian ministers, lawyers, writers…

I just didn't know anything about my great-aunt, Margaret Fuller, until many years later. Nobody ever played up the Fullers' intellectual side; Aunt Margaret was just somebody in the family to me.

Emerson was very much accepted and celebrated as a poet and essayist in my school, so I did know about him. But I didn't know about the extraordinary influence my own Aunt Margaret had had on him.

Father (top left)
Great-aunt
Margaret Fuller

She persuaded him that he ought to be published, and together they founded *Dial,* the prototype of the "little magazine" that she edited. *Dial* became the official magazine of the Transcendentalist movement, and under her editorship Thoreau and many others were first published and became known.

Aunt Margaret was a literary critic on the staff of the *New York Herald* and became the first woman foreign correspondent. Feminist, social reformer, writer—she did everything.

When she was in Italy she married the Marchese Giovanni Angelo Ossoli and they both took part in the Italian revolution under Mazzini. She was lost with her husband and child in a shipwreck off Fire Island.

Emerson

I was once reading Goethe and I came across a book in the library called *Margaret Fuller and Goethe*. I was fascinated to discover my Aunt Margaret. And once when I was lecturing at Wesleyan University about ten years ago, a professor from Oxford came up to me and gave me a poem:

> Fuller is the name, for better or for worse,
> Of two who grappled with the universe.
> "I'll accept it," said Margaret the spinster;
> "I'll explain it," said bold Buckminster.

Of course, Margaret was married to that Italian marchese, but it wouldn't rhyme that way.

I thought her essay, "Women in the Nineteenth Century," was so important that I published it in my book, *Ideas and Tensegrities*.

When I heard that Aunt Margaret said, "I must start with the universe and work down to the parts, I must have an understanding of it," that became a great drive for me.

I saw that in my education I was being pushed to be a specialist—everybody is being pushed to specialize, to where they can't be synergetic and can only know about the parts instead of the whole—I switched very vigorously; very deliberately, I became a comprehensivist.

Bear Island

Summers we spent on Bear Island in Penobscot Bay where we were one of two families living there. It was very primitive. Bear Island still is very primitive.

Father

I was about nine when my father persuaded Grandma Andrews—my mother's mother—to buy Bear Island, ten miles out from the mainland.

Before I had my glasses, and I couldn't see accurately, I really didn't understand the water. I could feel it, but I couldn't see its edge. It was very mystifying to me. I loved the feeling, but it was like being put in a bathtub and not really understanding it.

I remember my mother taking me into the water in Marblehead, and I was really, tremendously afraid. She couldn't understand why and she'd try to put me down, but I was afraid because I couldn't see where I was.
And when suddenly I could see, it was so exciting. To see things floating was incredible to me, with the light coming from underneath.
Our island had plenty of driftwood and timber, and I didn't have to ask anyone's permission to experiment with making boats that floated. I was amazed that such big heavy things as boats could float.

Most of the islands were completely uninhabited, and going around in my little boat I got to know all the fishermen-farmers. They were tremendously ingenious at making their own tools and their boats, combining the arts of the sea and the land. Well, I grew up with the idea of cutting my own trees and building my own boats.

Summers at
Bear Island

'My first
invention' — a
playpen for
Rosie

My first teleological invention was a mechanical "jellyfish." It was a tepee-like, folding, web-and-sprit cone, mounted like an inside-out umbrella on the submerged end of the pole.

The pole could be hand-pulled through a ring over the stern, drawing the self-folding cone through the water with little resistance. When the cone was pushed by the pole, it opened and gave inertial advantage, almost as though touching the bottom.

I could push-pull the boat along far more swiftly and easily than by sculling. Since I often used the boat in heavy fog and across strong currents, the push-pole also made it possible for me to maintain a forward watchfulness.

The old captain on our island taught me about ropes in our sailing boat, how you make things up and how you coil up the ropes because if you suddenly get a gust of wind you're going to have to do something in a hurry; you must never tie a knot—put a hitch on a cleat—but don't tie anything, it must be free for running, absolutely.
Because once you're in a blow, the ship goes over, the sea comes in, you won't swamp if you let go one of the sheets to ease the mainsail, but if the ropes are all mixed you're through!

... cutting my own trees, building my own boat...

Put everything where it belongs. Not because it's pretty, but because it's dangerous not to. Housekeeping, housekeeping, housekeeping!

This whole dealing with nature calls for alertness and a constant awareness and consciousness of nature. This is an environment not only for thinking, but for quick thinking. You learn you've got to make decisions quick or it's all over. Nature takes you to the bottom awful fast.

One of the single most important things I began to learn in my life on Bear Island was that we had a tide that came in and went out, a ten-foot tide. I'm a little tiny guy, but I could handle big things by virtue of that tide.

All the summers of my boyhood were spent here on the Bay. The route we're rowing along now is the same route I took every day to get the mail two miles away—over to Eagle Island and back.

love the sound of oars.
It just goes on and on
So I can keep on thinking without even realizing that I'm rowing—
any more than that I'm breathing.
Rowing is just as natural to me as breathing.

I bought this boat recently. It may be the last boat I will ever buy, and I hope
it's going to be the best boat in the world. I gave it the name *Intuition,* that
really being the key to thinking.

We do whatever things come spontaneously to us,
then suddenly, we're aware of thought.
We don't really know what made us say, "What was that?"
"y' see," or "I forgot that."
Intuition is our contact between conscious and subconscious.
It's your subconscious that suddenly comes through and lets you know
"this is something important to be thought about."
It's intuition that is continually opening doors of thought.

*Intuition — the key
to thinking.*

Sailing ships are extraordinary. A sailing ship opens up the sea, but unlike
bulldozer it doesn't hurt the sea. The sea closes in again. It gets from here
there without taking anything out of the energy wealth of the universe.

Then a very sad thing happened. My father had a series of strokes in three years—and suddenly he couldn't do anything on his own. Here was the father I loved and worshipped, the most incredibly loving man, and I was leading him around by the hand. That was a strange experience for a kid.

He died when I was quite young, and I missed his warmth. As long as he was alive we had all those amazing things, but when he died we couldn't have it; but my mother tried to carry on as if I were still a rich man's son.

Father's last visit to Bear Island, with me on the left, mother, brother Wooly, right, and baby Rosie.

The Milton football team in 1911, with me at left, front row.

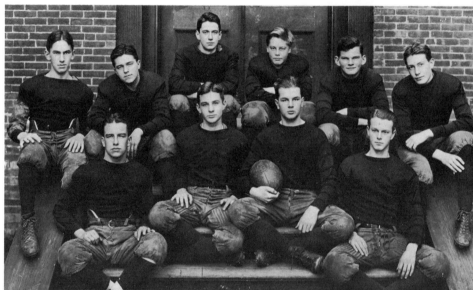

At any rate, I was now the oldest boy and I had to do all kinds of things around the house, like running the furnace and cleaning the rugs. I learned great deal about housekeeping—don't forget this was before anyone ever heard of carpet sweepers let alone vacuum cleaners.

I used to take the rugs out to the clothesyard and beat them by hand over lines and brush them and groom them. It really gave me a strong sense about the house and what you can be up against in cold rooms.

I went to Milton Academy where there was a boarding school, but I was a day scholar. There were very few of us day scholars, and you were then a little bit of a second-class kind of character because people realized you didn't have the kind of money needed to buy athletic gear—and I was very athletic, I loved the feeling and wanted to try my body, so I became a good athlete.

Official photo as
a Harvard man

In 1912 I became the fifth generation of Fullers to be accepted at Harvard. When I was at Milton Academy I dreamed of Harvard, but it turned out not to be the place where I was going to get an education after all.

I found that all my contemporaries from Milton Academy came into all the important Harvard clubs. Brooks Atkinson, who was in my class at Harvard, said he came there from Natick and none of his friends were going to be in any clubs...nor did they even think about it.
But my sister Leslie, who was three years older and married to a Porcellian man around the time I was in my freshman year in Harvard, told me, ''Bucky, you're going to be a disgrace to the family. You're not going to get into any of the clubs, and all the Milton boys are.''

But I didn't have an older brother or a father who would arrange things for me so that I would be admitted to one of the clubs on campus and do all the things the others did—they were all arranged.

Even my friends would come to me and say, ''Sorry Bucky, my brother says I can't play around with you anymore 'cause you're not going into a club.'' It was a horrid feeling. It hurt me terribly to find my friends being sorry for me. Then, too, I had my first falling-in-love and was jilted. So I felt hurt in several ways. And—it seems absolutely puerile today—I began showing off. I didn't want to be belittled by them.

"Stagedoor Johnny"

My sister Leslie had a Russian wolfhound, Mitzi. Leslie went off with her husband to live in Honolulu and she asked me to take care of her wolfhound in Cambridge because my mother had sold the Milton house. I discovered that all I had to do was stop at a theater stage door with my Russian wolfhound and every girl coming out of the theater would stop to see and pat this beautiful dog. So I could arrange very quickly, if they weren't engaged, to take them out to supper.

Now I was making all my classmates jealous of my being able to get these girls while they weren't able to get near them. There was a show then, the *Passing Show of 1912*—not Ziegfeld, but a sort of competitor of his called White. He had an actress and *premiere* danseuse and her name was Marilyn Miller.

Marilyn Miller

She wasn't the chief attraction; she was part of the variety show, but she was really charming and I liked her the most. So she fell for my Mitzi. She had a professional mother who traveled with her and they both agreed to have dinner with me at the Touraine Hotel—one of the fancy restaurants in Boston at that time. And I would show off with her.
Then her *Passing Show* went off to New York. That occurred just at the time of my mid-year exams. So I said I'm going down to New York with the show, and cut all my exams.

Marilyn Miller really did like me. I was her first stagedoor Johnny. After that she became a great star, and many men fell in love with her. I finally took the whole chorus out to dinner at Churchill's and used up my whole second year's allowance at one shot.

ell, Harvard couldn't do anything else but fire me—officially for cutting asses, but in fact for general irresponsibility.
nat really hurt my mother and she called a family conference with all my ncles to decide what was to be done with the black sheep of the family. ney said, "Never mind what *you* think. We know the real world, and you'd etter shape up!"
ney shipped me off to a cousin who had a cotton mill in Sherbrooke, uebec, where I was an apprentice millwright. I loved the people and e work.

earned to assemble and install every kind of cotton-mill machine—mostly nported in those days. This involved me in a self-tutored course of enineering exploration to rediscover what was behind the original designer's rategy in determining the designs of the various parts. I was even able to nprove on some and redesign them.

Vell, my mother really wanted me to go back to school and I reapplied at Harvard, was readmitted, and just as quickly, redismissed.
wasn't that I didn't do well in my studies—I received honors in biology, nathematics, and physics—but I was bored. I didn't like memorizing things nd felt it was a waste of my capabilities.

nd from left, apprentice millright Fuller

At the Naval Academy

Of my class of 700, only 45 were there for graduation. World War I broke out and everybody went off to war. I joined the Navy, and I was really upset with myself, because this was a war and people were getting killed—and here I was having the time of my life. Most of my friends thought serving in the Army and Navy was a chore, but I was absolutely in love with the Navy, because here I had bigger and better ships.

At the beginning of my naval service I was in charge of the boats guarding the works where the first naval aviation experimental development took place.
Many of our pilots would come in, make a bad landing, and trip and end up in the water, belted in and upside down. If I could get to them in time, our boys would jump overboard and try to cut them loose before they drowned. My boat was quite large, and I invented and had installed a powerful winch to pull the airplanes out of the water in a hurry while the boys pulled the pilot loose.

I was then sent to the United States Naval Academy. Then I became involved in the great transport operations that moved millions of people and supplies across the oceans of the world. This got me to thinking very big. I found the Navy was thinking in terms of the total world, of global planning, and that was an extraordinary experience for me.

In the Navy communications and events were logged chronologically, as they happened; and I began to realize the tremendous value of such records. So I began to think in terms of comprehensivity and continuity. I arranged my own records in chronological order and called it Chronofile. I said, I'm going to keep a record of things whether they are pleasing or not, and it turned out to be a valuable memory source.

Many years later, when I was science and technology consultant for *Fortune*, researchers from *Time* would come into my room and say, ''Bucky, you have a way of getting hold of remote things. Have you got anything on this or that? I can't find anything about it.'' I had my Chronofile bound in volumes, and I'd start working up and down the shelves. Suddenly, I'd find the answer that I listed fifteen years earlier. It's a very good memory mechanism.

Chief Boatswain Fuller at the helm of the USS Wego, the family boat volunteered for coast guard duty in Maine with the Navy Scout Patrol

In the Navy at last — bad eyes and all!

I remember the first time ever looking back at the wake of my ship and seeing all the whiteness and the foam,
and thinking, "That's white because it all consists of bubbles";
and I thought, "How many bubbles am I looking at?
I am looking at fantastic numbers of bubbles."
Here comes this wave.
Look at all this whiteness and all those bubbles. I said to myself, "I've been taught at school that to be able to design a model—because a bubble is a sphere—you have to use π, and the number, π, 3.14159265, on and on goes the number.
We find it cannot be resolved because it is a transcendental irrational.
So I said, "When nature makes one of those bubbles, how many places did she have to carry out π
before she discovered you can't resolve it? And at what point does nature decide to make a fake bubble?"
I said, "I don't think nature is turning out any fake bubbles, I think nature's not using π."
This made me start looking for ways in which nature did contrive all mensu rations, all her spontaneous associations,
without using such numbers.

*At Armour picnic,
sans glasses, but with
new moustache.*

When I came out of the Navy I went into Armour and Co.'s great packing
house. They made me assistant export manager. I began thinking about the
total foods of humanity around the world.

You see how by this comprehensive anticipatory way of looking at things
and thinking about the total needs of total man, I came a few years later to
invent the words, "Spaceship Earth." Because I began to think about the total
planet as being as beautifully designed and equipped as a ship.

How do you run it in such a way as to take care of everybody?

Nobody was thinking of it in those terms, and I said they should be doing just that. The Navy meant, not only getting into the air with airplanes and into the ocean with ships and submarines, but into radio which was really just developing. I was very excited when one of the boats I was commanding was assigned to Dr. Lee DeForest to make the first experiment of talking by voice radio from an airplane to a ship at sea. I felt I was being introduced to a new world. Later, I became an aide to admirals in charge of the 130 transports and cruisers moving millions of people across the ocean and back. I kept track of all shipping movements and I became deeply involved in communications.

When President Wilson went to Paris at the end of the war, for the peace conference, he was the first president in history to use radio. We arranged for him to be able to communicate all the way across the Atlantic. I was there when the first transoceanic telephone call was made by Wilson from the steamship *George Washington* to Arlington.

It was through experiences like this that I was discovering what was going on in technology. This breaking down of great distances on earth and in the sky was something so foreign to anything my father or my grandfather or my great-grandfather ever experienced.

I began to realize we were in acceleration in human affairs too,
that a new world was coming in.
We were going from track to trackless,
from wire to wireless…to ephemeralization.
I began to realize that while armies fight very local battles,
the Navy is inherently comprehensive, dealing with the total earth.

After the second time I was fired from Harvard I went down to New York, where I met this lovely girl, Anne Hewlett. I courted her through thick and thin for two years and she came to visit me at the Naval Academy in Annapolis in 1917. We were married July 12 at Rock Hall, Long Island—with all the trimmings.

The wedding cake was enormous and I cut the first slice with my sword. In the excitement I replaced the sword in its scabbard, cake-crusted. Some time after that I was embarrassed when I drew my sword to find wedding-cake crumbs still stuck to it.

Anne came from a large family; she was the oldest of ten children. Her father, James Monroe Hewlett, was a prominent architect and he introduced me to the world of architecture. For the first time I met people who were building on the land. And for the first time there was a father again, who said to me, "Don't pay attention to what people say. What you think is the most important thing. Pay attention to your own thoughts."

James Monroe Hewlett

Our first child Alexandra was born at the end of World War I. She caught the flu, then spinal meningitis, and finally infantile paralysis. She had a wonderful mind, as all children do, and wanted information, but she couldn't walk around because of her illness. Every little child wants to stand up and go over and verify what she sees, and touch it and be sure what it really is; continually confirming the information it's getting from its other senses.

She was terribly sensitive to what was said, so that we were often astonished by her response. Two of us would be in the room with her, and we would start to say something having no connection with the kind of thing anyone would talk to a child about. For example, I would talk about some responsibility I had outside the house. And just as I was about to speak, I would be absolutely astonished to find my own words coming out of her mouth.

Alexandra

Anne

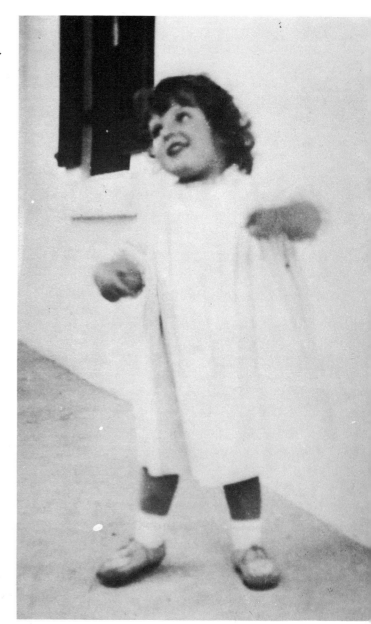

I can only say that there is something like telepathy going on around us, which I am convinced will ultimately be identified as ultra-ultra-high-frequency electromagnetic waves. But because we have no proof of its existence, we try to brush it aside.

Alexandra died in 1923, and I couldn't help feeling somehow responsible, that if she had had a proper environment she would have lived.
I began to drink heavily. I also threw myself into my work.
In the early 20s, my father-in-law invented a building system of recycled celotexlike blocks mixed with cement, and that brought me directly into the building world. We set up the Stockade Building Company and went into business together. I found it to be a very different game from the one I had learned in the Navy.

When I was in the Navy, everything went great because all I had to do was run a good ship, keep it on top of the water, and get done what had to be done. I didn't have to make money with it. Suddenly, with my father-in-law, I had gotten into the building world, and I discovered that what they were doing was trying to make money with building, rather than make good buildings.
What hit me very hard was that the building world was thousands of years behind the art of designing ships of the sea and the air. On land, for instance, the thicker and heavier walls were constructed, the more secure people felt —exactly the opposite of doing more with less. At sea and in the sky you had to do more with less.

The Stockade Company was based in Joliet, Illinois where they have that great Illinois penitentiary, and I drove there every day from Chicago where we were living.

I drove through Cicero to get to work and it was a constant reminder of Al Caponeworld. I was drinking then—it was during Prohibition when even a beer was illegal—but wherever I'd stop for a drink the place'd belong to Capone.

It seems we were always coming in on scenes with gangsters. Just getting of a trolley once coming up State Street there was a shooting in the cathedral. Even in the hall of our apartment on Belmont, Anne would meet this guy in the hall with his coat open and guns showing in his holsters.

And he was always so polite to her, and so helpful.

Then I'd go out at night with some of the company's stockholders, the richest of all Chicagoans with enormous amounts of money, and the night spot was owned by gangsters—another Capone spot.

I got into bad habits of dealing in rich people's places. My salary as head of Stockade Company was $50 a week, so it wasn't easy to carry on.

I was really working very hard, long hours, opening 5 new factories and 24 or so buildings. I thought we were doing well. But my father-in-law sold his stock to raise money he needed and the new people didn't think the company was making a big enough profit. So I was pushed out by the new management. I was a complete failure at business and we were left stranded in Chicago.

The death of Alexandra just before her fourth birthday in 1923 and the

The Stockade Building Company in Joliet

failure of the building company in 1927 marked a low point in the Fuller
fortunes. I had started drinking quite a lot when my daughter died and
now everything seemed to be going wrong. I had no idea what I was going
to do next. I was absolutely broke. How were we going to eat?

All the things that I had been taught worked, were true, but were on a colli-
sion course. And all because I wasn't going according to my own thinking
but was following everyone else's criteria.
I was in a mess. Finally I reached a point where I found myself saying, "Am I
an utter failure? If so I'd better get myself out of the way."

But I said to myself, "You do not belong to you, therefore you do not have
the right to eliminate yourself. You belong to the universe."
I used to wander aimlessly in the city, and take long walks around the lake,
just drifting about.

It was in 1927 that I had this really extraordinary experience, the only
one that ever happened to me that was really and utterly mystical.

At that time Henry Ford was exhibiting his Model A, down at the Armory,
having switched from the Model T, so I walked down from Belmont Avenue.

I was on Michigan Avenue, about three or four blocks south of the Chicago
River, right across from the Wrigley Building,
when suddenly I found myself with my feet not touching the pavement;
I found myself in a sort of sparkling kind of sphere....

I couldn't believe it.
And I heard a voice, such as I had never heard, ever before, saying,
"From now on you need never await temporal attestation to your thought.
You think the truth."

I couldn't believe I was not touching the ground
and that I was hearing this extraordinary thing!
It was after that that I started writing feverishly.
I said, "I think I must write everything down,
because I was thinking the truth."

There were thoughts about everything.
And I said, "Now who would be interested in this thought?" and I'd make an
envelope and say, "I believe Bob Sherwood would be interested,"
and I sorted out all my thoughts that way.
Then, when I had all these envelopes, I said, "I must write these people a
letter incorporating everything in their envelopes." I did this, and then I cut
the names off, and later they became the chapters for *4D Timelock*.

And it was also in 1927 that I was inspired by the birth of a new child, Allegra.

Lincoln Park in Chicago, with Anne and Allegra who is just learning to walk.

Mother, Anne, and Allegra, at far right, off Bear Island.

I had good cause with our first child to feel that children are endowed with a great deal more than many of us know, that every child may be born a genius but may simply be degeniused at an early age because parents and environment lack the ability to recognize these faculties.

I said, "I'm really going to give the rest of my life to the new young life." I pledged, both to the daughter who died and to the daughter now born, that I was committing myself to humanity.

1927–1977:
FIFTY-YEAR EXPERIMENT

Realizing that there was nobody to tell me to undertake a comprehensive design science, I decided to become the prime designer myself!

In 1927, I resolved to do my own thinking, and see what the individual, star ing without any money or credit—in fact, with considerable discredit, but with a whole lot of experience—to see what the individual, with a wife an new-born child, could produce on behalf of his fellow men.

I said, "What can a little man effect toward such realizations in the face of the formidable power of great corporations, great states, and all their know-how, guns, monies, armies, tools and information?"
Then, self-answering: "The individual can take initiatives without anybody's permission." Only individuals can think, and can look for the principles manifest in their experiences that others may be overlooking because they are too preoccupied with how to please some boss or with how to earn money, how to take care of today's bills.

Only the individual disregards his fears and commits himself exclusively to reforming the human environment by developing tools that deal more effec tively and economically with evolutionary challenges.
Humans can participate—consciously and competently—in fundamental ways, to changes that are more favorable to human life.
It became evident that the individual was the only one that could deliber- ately find the time to think in a cosmically adequate manner.

This was to be a fifty-year experiment
to prove that man, like nature, was not a failure but a success;
to rethink everything I knew.
It was an experiment in which I myself was the guinea pig.
I had to begin from the beginning.
I had to find out what man has
and see how it can be used for the advantage of others.
I became convinced that we're here for each other.

Once I'd committed myself to that kind of program I had to expand what I'd
already learned by a great deal, and unlearn a great deal that I had been
taught was so that I'd found out was not so. And that was the most difficult
discipline I took on.
I scarcely spoke at all for two years. I couldn't be completely free of words,
but my wife had to talk to people for me. I didn't want to say anything, make
any sounds, until I was pretty sure what those sounds meant and why I
wanted to use them. I had to make a complete disconnect in order to start
my own thinking.

I said,
"How do we find out how to use our minds and experience
to the highest advantage of others in the shortest possible time?"
That was the challenge.
Out of this then, in due course, came a great many designs,
because I said to myself,
"I must commit myself to reforming the environment
and not man;
being absolutely confident that if you give man the right environment
he will behave favorably."
By employing the kinds of capabilities used in building a battleship,
you do more with less.
I'm convinced that by more with lessing we could take care of everybody
and there need not be any suffering around the world.

My first intuition was the possibility
that in my experience there were the means of helping others
avoid the pain I felt.

By the age of 32,
I had inadvertently acquired a widely variegated background
of technical, scientific, naval-construction, management,
and economic experience
which spontaneously produced my experience
that all physical problems could best be solved by a competent arrangemer
of the constituents of the environment
in such a manner as to be productive for all humanity.

My five years with the Stockade convinced me that no company out to
make money could bring the kind of technological improvements to the
building world that I had experienced during the war in the Navy. Because
of that, people aren't able to buy houses the way they buy cars.

Money is absolutely irrelevant.
What is relevant is man and his environment and his time,
and you can get the environment to begin to work with you.
I wanted to give my child the maximum chance
so that it wouldn't be misinformed,
so it would be able to get all the information it wants and needs
in order to be able to understand its universe
and to be able to operate Spaceship Earth properly within that universe.

Here I was, a failure.
I decided man was operating on a fundamental fallacy:
that man was supposed to be a failure
and therefore had to prove his right to live.
Each man then said,
"I must show I can earn my living, and let other people go die."
I decided the fallacy was that man was, in fact, designed
to be an extraordinary success.
His characteristics were just magnificent; what was needed
was to discover the comprehensive patterns operating in the universe.
The universe is a success.
How could metaphysical man, using his mind, master the physical?

Clearly, the possibility of a good life for any man
depends upon the possibility of realizing it for all men.

I must be able to convert the resources of the earth,
doing more with less,
until I reach a point where we can do so much
as to be able to service all men in respect to all their needs.

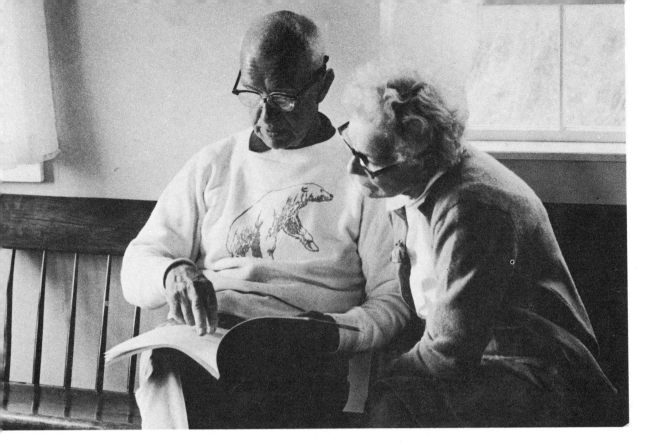

With sister Rosie at Bear Island

I found that one of the things I needed to do was saturate myself with information. Saturate. Because out of information come generalized principles. Only man has the ability to deal in generalized principles.

The brain is part of man's physical equipment. It has so many cubbyholes... every experience he has, man puts into his memory bank.
The memory bank is the brain. But I differentiate between mind and brain very distinctly. Mind, and mind alone, reviews the total inventory of experiences. From time to time man finds something running through all of them.

Suppose, for instance, you had a stack of punchcards, all the same perimeter size, say 4"x 5", full of holes.
They look very random to you and me, but stack them all up vertically, with guides to the edges, and put a light alongside them and you see two holes which light comes through. These two holes are constant to every card. This is typical; we call it "generalized principle"—it holds true in every case.

It is an absolutely abstract phenomenon, and, as far as we can find out, animals don't employ generalized principles.

Generalizations in language are sometimes used to cover too much territory too thinly, but generalizations used in science—scientific generalizations—are principles that have been discovered to hold true in every case. They never fail.

For instance:

A man is walking through a forest where many trees have been felled by great storms. He walks along on a tree to get from one spot to another... from here to there. The tree slowly begins to sink, and he says:

"What's going on here?" and retreats.

Then he gets back on it and again it goes down slowly.

He notices that the tree is lying across another tree, and the other end of the tree he's on is under a great big tree. He goes over and tries to lift it, and he says:

"I can't lift a tree like that, but every time I go over here, that big tree is lifting."

So he says:

"I think I've got a magic tree."

He drags it home and everybody worships it.

But pretty soon his wife says:

"I think any tree will do."

And this is a generalization of the principle of leverage.

Suppose I take a piece of rope and tense it, very, very vigorously.
It becomes taut—that is, the rope contracts and gets harder and harder;

which means that at 90 degrees to my tensing it, the rope is getting into compression—we are discovering a generalized principle of tension and compression.

Many architects mistakenly talk about using tension all by itself—but there's always compression occurring at 90 degrees to the tensing.

For instance, imagine a number of steel rods, round rods of the same size, each one so slender it bends very easily.

Now, I take a bunch of them and compact them as tightly as I can—I get them into the hexagon/honeycomb pattern, which is called closest packing. They can't get any closer together.

Now I put some bands around them, like this—wrap them together—and load the whole of them as a group, a column, from the top here. The rods can't bend toward each other, because they're already packed the closest they can get. They can only bend away from each other.

There's nothing stopping them from opening that way, except that there are some bands around them. So I load this column, and like a cigar its girth tries to keep stretching and gets fatter and fatter.

As it gets fatter and fatter, its girth goes into tension. So while I am purposely loading—compression—it goes into tension at 90 degrees again.

So we find tension and compression always and only coexisting.

If I keep on loading such a column, it will finally become a sphere.

Nature has spheres—the earth, the moon, and the atoms—all islands of compression possessing great integrity, held together entirely by an invisible web of tension.

Tension is discontinuous; compression is continuous.
I call this tensional integrity; and I've shortened that to "tensegrity."

A poem that came out of World War I ends with the line:
"But only God can make a tree."
It is interesting that we can now discern how a tree is made, how it works.

In nature's designing, there is a very low tensile strength in gases; a little higher tensile strength in liquids; and highest in solids. In designing her tree nature to a certain extent works as we did in developing the automobile and the airplane:
You couldn't have that great piece of machinery weighing two tons
go over a road, even a very well developed cement road,
without completely cracking up if it had hard, crystalline wheels.
So we developed the pneumatic tire, which distributes all the loads applied to it to the whole tensile surface of the tire,
and very great shock is absorbed from it due to the fact that those gases are compressible, distributing the loads.

When an airplane comes down out of the sky,
a hundred tons come down,
hitting the earth at 200 miles an hour with 200 tons,
and boy! that is really quite a trick;
not only does it have pneumatic tires, it has the hydraulic strut.
And because the liquids are noncompressible, the hydraulic strut forces the liquids through a number of channels
and takes an enormous part of the load, reducing the working load.

The tree is designed exactly that way.
Nature ships the seed from here to there by air;
the instructions are to build a tree
and to count on local gases and liquids available—
in fact, the tree won't take root unless there are liquids available.
When the seed arrives, it gets the instruction to all the crystallines and fibers
to go into tension.
All the compression is done by liquids within the fibers.
The gases take the shock loads,
because between the molecules there are gases.

The tree holding out its arm, the ring root of the tree that goes off to this
great branch is a great matter.
If you try lifting a 50-pound suitcase while holding your arm out horizontally,
you'll find you can't do it.
But a tree is often holding out a branch weighing as much as five tons.
Holding five tons out there horizontally,
and being able to do so in a hurricane, is perfectly extraordinary.
The tree does this so as to hold out those leaves so they'll be able to take in
enough energy from the sun to keep the life going on our earth,
because that is its function.

The tree does this by virtue of the high tensile strength in the crystalline
which makes the fibers and the sap;
the liquids then act as a noncompressive, but do distribute the loads, so that
the tree can also impound the sun's radiation and not be dehydrated,
so that life can be regenerated by the sun's radiation, and
other creatures can eat the many parts of the vegetation.

The tree has to have roots so it won't be dehydrated, so it takes enormous
amounts of water by osmosis.
Tons and tons of water are being lifted out of the earth and into the sky.
While that water is impounded inside the system, it is noncompressible,
an absolutely beautiful thing,
so it can handle this load without compressing and it can distribute the load
to all of its parts.

All the parts in it are working together: the gas molecules between each of
the hydraulic molecules are the shock load,
so that when the wind hits it, it can yield, swaying, like that.
Now the minute you have an ice storm, those molecules go all crystalline, it
can't distribute all its loads, and down go all the branches.
Nature's principles are employed in the most logical way, and the tree can
do tasks that men are unable to do.

A human being is what I call a pattern integrity.

I'm going to take a piece of manila rope, and then I'm going to splice into a piece of cotton rope. I splice into the other end of the cotton rope a piece of nylon rope. I'm going to make the very simplest knot I know, whic is to go around 360 degrees in this plane and 360 degrees in that plane.

I'm not going to pull it tight. There's the knot.

The rope has not done this, I have done it to the rope. At any rate, I can slide it along…and now it's on the nylon—suddenly, it's off the end. We sa "The knot was a pattern integrity." It wasn't manila, it wasn't cotton, it wasr nylon.
Cotton, nylon, and manila—any one of them is good to let us know its shap what its pattern was; but it wasn't that: it had an integrity of its own.

"...just yesterday's cereal..."

I took off seventy pounds recently because I was overweight.
Who was that? It wasn't me!
I have taken on over 1,000 tons of food, air, and water
since I was born,
and I am not any of that poundage at all.
When I die I will still be somewhere around 140 pounds—
and you can throw that away, because
that's just yesterday's cereal.

Another generalized principle is that of wave behavior.

I drop a stone in the water and a most beautiful circular wave emanates. I then try it on milk, on kerosene, and it works just as well.
And the next thing I say is: "I'd like to know about that. Apparently that wave isn't just water and it isn't just milk."

So I try sprinkling sawdust all over the water very neatly, and make a beautiful film of sawdust. Then I drop one piece of red popcorn on that. I put a transit and a moving-picture camera very carefully aimed at that red popcorn.

I drop the stone—over here—in the water, and the yellow sawdust makes a wave.

Suddenly the red popcorn goes out from the center of the earth, in toward the center, and comes right back where it was. It simply went in and out to accommodate the wave, to let it go by, just as the piece of rope accommodated the knot sliding along on it.

All systems as viewed from the inside are concave; viewed from the out-side, they are convex.
Convex and concave are not the same, because concave converges and conserves energy and convex distributes it. Concave pulls the radiation to-gether, and convex diffuses it.

So, they are not the same: there is not the same energy effect. Yet they always and only coexist.
We have the proton and the neutron which always and only coexist.

So now we have three always-and-only coexisting phenomena: tension and compression, concave and convex, proton and neutron.

Now I come back to what I started off with. I said, "I have a piece of rope and I'm tensing it," and I didn't have a piece of rope at all. And nobody ever says, "You don't have a piece of rope!" This is what I call a first-degree generalization.

Everybody in the audiences has had experience with ropes, many, many pieces of ropes. And I just say "cotton" or "nylon" or whatever it is, and I find that as long as I don't contradict the experience all of them have had with rope, they will generalize from their experience.

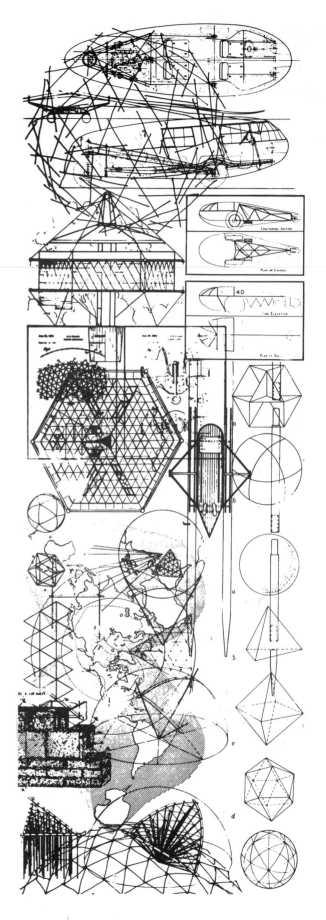

In considering the idea of applying generalized principles to the home front,
I saw that the universe is ever and forever continually intertransforming,
following a number of rules
and a number of alternate ways in which it can transform.
So I said—I must understand how to produce artifacts
out of the intertransforming of nature's energy.
This brought me to a whole series of inventions,
or what I call trial balances—
checking out my theories against reality.
I didn't set out to do these things. I was applying nature's generalized
principles.

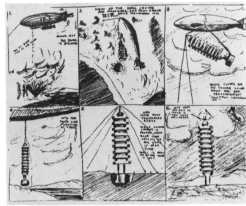

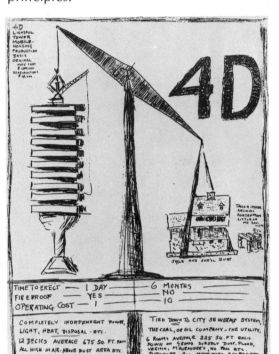

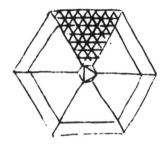

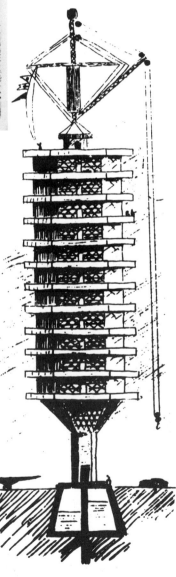

The 4D Tower House grew out of my book of essays *4D Timelock* and my
design for a four-dimensional Tower House.

I was thinking then of housing as shelters that could be mass-produced and
delivered as finished dwellings to any place its owner wanted it to be;
this ten-deck building was designed to be so light and so strong that it could
have been carried by the *Graf Zeppelin,* which was then being built, and
was perfectly flyable economically to the North Pole where it could be
anchored.

Conventional buildings, constructed stone on stone, are almost completely
compression structures and weigh as much as when they built the pyramids.
The 4D Tower House was stressed like airplanes, with compression and
tension parts separated out—again, of continuous tension and discontinuous compression, with compression islands floating in a tension web.

I then gave myself the task of designing a building that would house an airplane maintenance crew and which could be installed in remote places, like the Arctic, so that we would have stepping-stone flights to Europe by way of the Arctic.

Stepping-stone flights to Europe

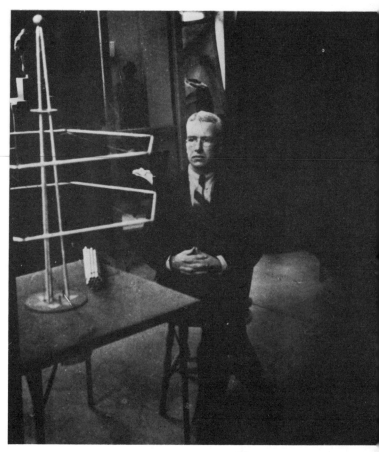

With early model of Dymaxion House

So, having proved the feasibility of flying a whole building,
I designed the 4D single-family dwelling the model of which was made for Marshall Field's House of the Future show.

Recently the editors of the Oxford Dictionary asked me to define Dymaxion. I said, "It means doing the most with the least."

Because they wanted a jazzier name for the house, the two advertising men made a list of words they heard me use in what they thought were my most important sentences. Then they took the key words and using the most prominent syllables of the most prominent words of the most prominent thoughts of mine, they made another list. I was permitted to throw out the most objectionable words.
We were left with dynamic, maximum, and ion, out which they fashioned "Dymaxion." Marshall Field made me a present of the name.

The 4D
Single Family
Dwelling

The Dymaxion House
looks like a house on a pole,
and simply because of its wire-wheel construction, it has less weight.
I turn the wire wheel over on its side—
and the hub is now a mast. The house is hexagonal, and has great space in it
for a family of five:
Good-size bedrooms, bath, large living room, utility room, library, sundeck
and hangar on top and, because it was raised one story, garage below.
The mast, which also held the basic utilities,
was factory-installed and ready for instant use.
The elevator was in the mast.

It was designed to be dustless, with air drawn in through vents in the mast, filtered, washed, cooled or heated, and then circulated. It had an automatic laundry, presser, drier and storage units. Clothes and dish closets and refrigerator and food compartments had revolving shelves adjusted to move at the interruption of a light beam.

Like a ship, it was almost entirely independent of piped-in water. It could be fully operative as soon as it was set down.

The bathroom I designed for the Dymaxion House was aimed at functionality and conservation. A ten-minute atomizer bath used a single quart of water which was filtered, sterilized, and recycled.

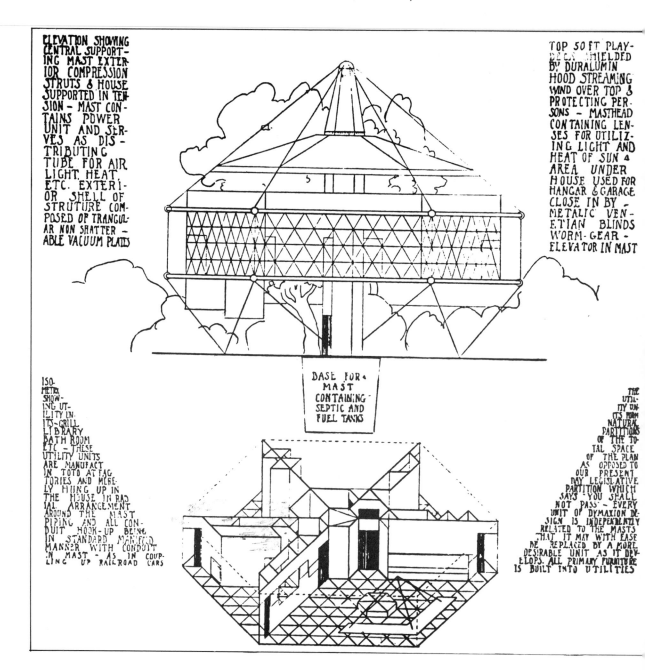

ELEVATION SHOWING CENTRAL SUPPORTING MAST EXTERIOR COMPRESSION STRUTS & HOUSE SUPPORTED IN TENSION - MAST CONTAINS POWER UNIT AND SERVES AS DISTRIBUTING TUBE FOR AIR LIGHT HEAT ETC. EXTERIOR SHELL OF STRUTURE COMPOSED OF TRIANGULAR NON SHATTER - ABLE VACUUM PLATES

TOP 50 FT PLAYDECK SHIELDED BY DURALUMIN HOOD STREAMING WIND OVER TOP & PROTECTING PERSONS - MASTHEAD CONTAINING LENSES FOR UTILIZING LIGHT AND HEAT OF SUN & AREA UNDER HOUSE USED FOR HANGAR & GARAGE CLOSE IN BY METALIC VENETIAN BLINDS WORM-GEAR ELEVATOR IN MAST

BASE FOR MAST CONTAINING SEPTIC AND FUEL TANKS

ISOMETRIC SHOWING UTILITY IN ITS-GRILL LIBRARY BATH ROOM ETC - THESE UTILITY UNITS ARE MANUFACT IN TOTO AT FACTORIES AND MERELY HUNG UP IN THE HOUSE IN RADIAL ARRANGEMENT AROUND THE MAST PIPING AND ALL CONDUIT HOOK-UP BEING IN STANDARD MANIFOLD MANNER WITH CONDUIT IN MAST - AS IN COUPLING UP RAILROAD CARS

THE UTILITY UNITS FORM NATURAL PARTITIONS OF THE TOTAL SPACE OF THE PLAN AS OPPOSED TO OUR PRESENT DAY LEGISLATIVE PARTITION WHICH SAYS - YOU SHALL NOT PASS - EVERY UNIT OF DYMAXION DESIGN IS INDEPENDENTLY RELATED TO THE MASTS THAT IT MAY WITH EASE BE REPLACED BY A MORE DESIRABLE UNIT AS IT DEVELOPS. ALL PRIMARY FURNITURE IS BUILT INTO UTILITIES

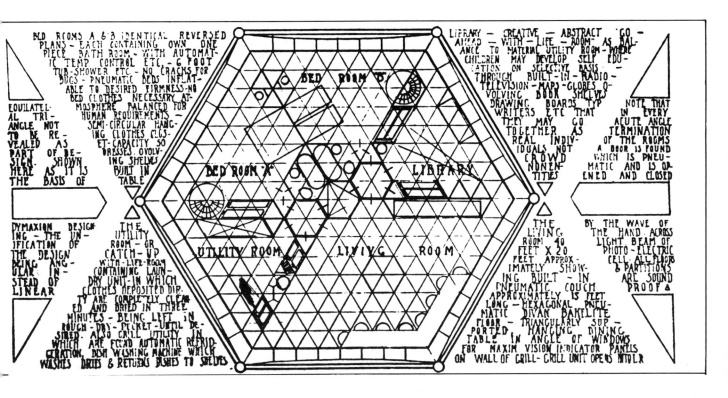

The toilets in my bathroom required no water, but consisted of a splashless, hermetic, and waterproof packaging system which packed, stored, and cartoned waste for future use by chemical industries.

The entire building weighed only three tons.

Taking the weight of an average so-called satisfactory single-family dwelling which the American Institute of Architects considered adequate for father, mother, and two children, I found the whole thing weighed 150 tons.

From 150 tons to three tons is quite a jump. But when, in 1928, I offered to assign all rights to the American Institute of Architects, they turned down the offer, being, as they said, "inherently opposed to any peas-in-a-pod reproducible designs."

But I could already see then that if everyone was to get high quality shelter, houses must be mass-produced industrially, in large quantities, like automobiles. At that time it cost little more per pound than a Ford did, or a Chevrolet—installed for living—through the use of mass-production techniques. And I could see that we might really be able to do more with less.

Bucky with a model of the Dymaxion House.

The kind of technology used as a matter of course in the ocean and the air —that went from pipe to pipeless, track to trackless, wire to wireless—why shouldn't it be adapted to land?

But I quickly realized that to make this possible I would have to wait for reasonably priced aluminum, plastics, and high-strength steel alloys that were not yet available.

Many people thought I was some kind of a nut because I was talking about air-conditioning, packaged kitchens, and built-in furniture. But there were some architects who didn't go along with the AIA and my image as some kind of wild man, and I began to get invitations to come and lecture about my ideas.

I decided to make a complete experiment of peeling off from society in general, and started wearing T-shirts which nobody was doing then, went about without a hat and in sneakers—absolutely comfortable clothes. Then when people started getting interested in my Dymaxion House, very nice people with influence, and they'd say, "I'd like to give a dinner party for you" and so forth, I would show up in khaki pants and they'd be very shocked. And when Mrs. John Alden Carpenter, head of the Arts Council in Chicago, gave a beautiful dinner party, I showed up and rudely announced, "I don't eat that kind of food," and was in every way obnoxious.

I was putting self and comfort ahead of my Dymaxion House, and I said, "You're not allowed to do that. You must get over that. You must stop that looking eccentric, with everybody pointing at this guy."

So I decided the way to do that was to become the invisible man, and that means a bank clerk—so I put on a black suit, bank clerk's clothing; then they would focus on what I was saying instead of my eccentricities. I said, "I must get rid of continually making too much of myself."

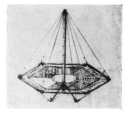

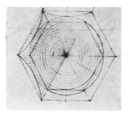

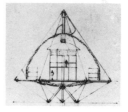

Dymaxion Mobile Dormitory (1931)

Greenwich Village Days

Anyway, by 1928 I was back in New York and I began to hang around in the Village. I used to go to Romany Marie's, a restaurant I was introduced to by a friend even before I went to Chicago. It was probably the last of the really great Bohemian cafés I know of in the world—very much like the Paris of the 20s. The Village was loaded then with great artists and great intellectuals, and Marie had by far the best place in town. That's where I carried on and developed my ideas. Certainly, in Greenwich Village they took me and my ideas seriously.

What I found so exciting there was that for the first time in my life I had a grand strategy and could try out my thinking against the best of the intellectuals.

Many intellectuals became communists, and I'd say about one-third of the people who came there regularly were communists. I was very apolitical and they were very political.

Romany Marie's

John Sloan

And they would give me a great battle, and a chance to defend my position. They would really battle me hard. It was probably one of the best conditionings I've ever had.
And they liked the Dymaxion House.
They didn't quite see how we could ever get it going, but they liked the feel of it.

After the great stockmarket crash in 1929 and the Depression that followed anyone could see that the economic system here in New York as well as everyplace else in America had broken down. People slept in subways; unemployment was everywhere. Some restaurants were down to one-cent meals, and you could buy a whole suit of clothes for a dollar.
Even at that, no one could sell anything. No one had any money!

They were fantastic times.

Romany Marie

I made some furniture to decorate Romany Marie's in the Village—she was then at Minnetta Lane—and she would give me a meal every day instead of money. She would keep a big pot of vegetable soup cooking all the time, constantly adding water and pieces of meat. It was delicious, but I didn't want to overdo it so I only came every other night. There I would stay, a table-sitter, all evening, until very late into the night. It was the Greenwich Village of the late '20s and early '30s that generated great new thinking— and I gained many friends for my concepts, and lost none.

Marie was very interested in me and my work. By this time she had moved her place to South Washington Square, down in a basement, and she ran it together with Puck Durant, Will's wife.

They asked me to have an exhibition of my Dymaxion House. I had a model, d'ye see, a beautiful model that I made for the Chicago show, and in the summer of 1929 I gave my talks down there.

"... This was Noguchi."

I met a young man there who had just come to New York from Europe where he'd been studying with Brancusi—and this was Noguchi.

"I first met Mr. Fuller, as I used to call him," said Noguchi, much later, "at Romany Marie's in 1929. Some time later I got an old laundry room on top of a builidng on Madison Avenue and 29th Street with windows all around. Under Bucky's sway I painted the whole place silver—so that one was almost blinded by the lack of shadows. There I made his portrait head in chrome-plated bronze—also form without shadow.

"Bucky was in a continuous state of dialectic creativity, giving talks in any situation before any kind of audience ... He would talk to me as though to a throng; walking and talking everywhere—over the Brooklyn Bridge, over innumerable cups of coffee. Bucky drank everything—tea, coffee, liquor—with equal gusto and would often be in a state of wide-awake euphoria for three days straight. Drink did not seem to affect him otherwise.

"He used to drink like a fish. He had become a God-possessed man, like a Messiah of ideas. He was a prophet of things to come. Bucky didn't take care of himself, but he had amazing strength. He often went without sleep for several days, and he didn't always eat either.

"Bucky's zest for life is part and parcel of his creativity. However, he has the capacity and resolution to come to grips in unknown hours and retreats of the mind to fathom new secrets from the universe."

He absolutely fell in love with that house and everything I said;
and he said, could he make a head of me?
and I said I'd be glad to have him do it.
So posing for him day after day gave us a chance to build up our friendship
that went on and on from there.

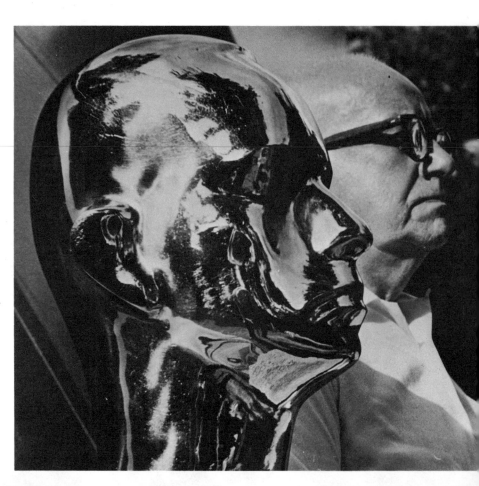

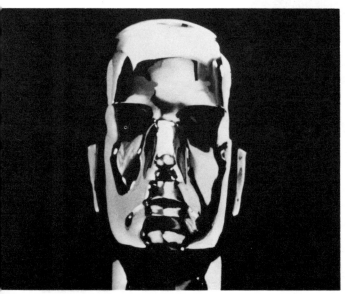

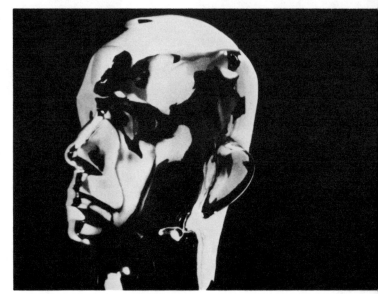

Noguchi used to do real well. He was a bachelor, and he always got big money for his commissions. He made these heads of the most beautiful people. So Isamu was OK; I was continually bust, and he used to let me sleep in his studio—usually on the floor.

When the Depression set in seriously and most of the New York hotels were empty and looking for something to attract people, they'd ask me to come with my Dymaxion house to be on exhibit. They would give me a beautiful room or apartment to use as an exhibition room and Isamu and I would sleep on the floor—no bedclothes or anything. They gave us a bathroom to go to, and we'd literally live on coffee and doughnuts every other day or so.

"We would move in with our air mattresses and a drawing board and that was it. The less the better was his credo. His Shelter *magazine was produced under such circumstances (1930–1932)," recalled Noguchi.*

It was really tough going. I had Anne and Allegra down in the country. My mother helped me a little with an allowance to look out for them; but I lived on the minimum you can possibly get on with.

In 1930, I sold all my life insurance and took over a magazine called *T-Square.* I changed its name to *Shelter,* and published it for the next two years—up to the '32 election of Franklin Roosevelt and his New Deal which followed the absolute disaster of the previous laissez-faire economy. With the New Deal's dedication to "the forgotten man," I decided to cease kibbitzing.

Allegra

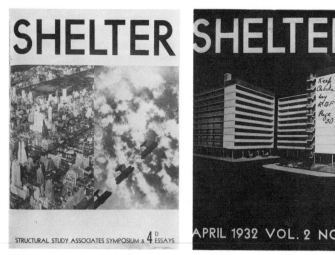

Shelter was quite a design-science adventure in itself. The first thing I did was to cast out all its previously lucrative advertising contracts. Publishers said that meant disaster.

But advertising contracts require that you bring out regular issues on regular dates. This means editorial deadlines. Deadlines mean sacrifice of the best and timeliest thinking. I notified the subscribers that thinking does its own timing and told them when I had something I felt deeply in need of saying I would do so, regardless of dates. I then told the subscribers that the luxury of saying what you thought when you thought it needed to be said would cost two dollars per copy—whereas *Fortune,* which also began in 1930, was charging the then unprecedented price of one dollar per copy.

I published anonymously, using the name 4D; and I gave space to people like Frank Lloyd Wright.

With Frank Lloyd Wright

By this time I was finding an enormous number of people who were acting as though I were some kind of new Christ or Messiah. I didn't like that at all. Krishnamurti was in the city and they were making *him* a Messiah, and I said, "That's fine, you can do that to him, but not me."

My mother died and I inherited some money and joined this racquet-tennis club in a very high-moving, fast-drinking world. I had made a New Year's resolution earlier to give up drinking, and it was going to be terrific because of the sense of freedom I had had from not drinking. I was then in a wonderful position because I said, "I'm literally jumping overboard; I know what a mess drinking really is." But then I started drinking again and did everything offensive to all the people who were trying to make me a Messiah. And I lost all the people who thought I was great.

In spite of the mess, I managed to write my first book, *Nine Chains to the Moon,* in 1935, which came out very well.

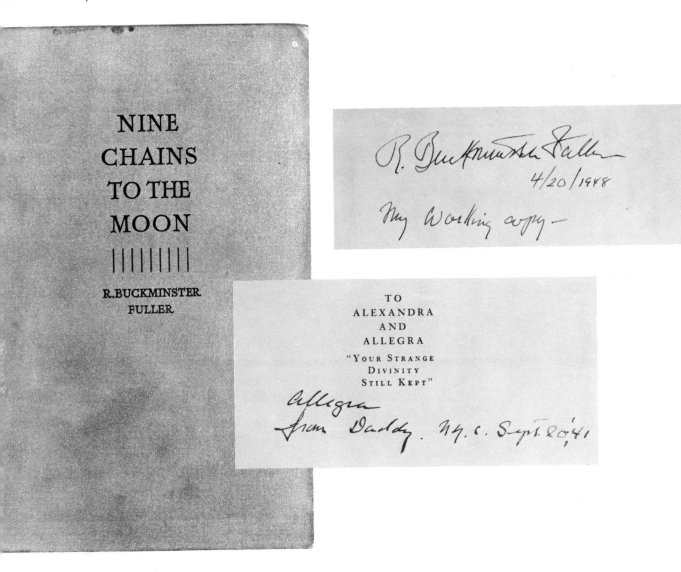

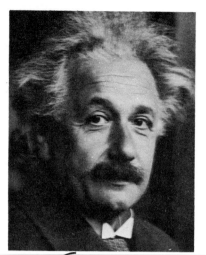

Einstein

The New York Times Magazine section of New Year's, 1930, had a lead article by Einstein called, "The Cosmic Religious Sense," a nonanthropomorphic concept of God, in which he also wrote that fear and longing were fundamental motivations of man. I thought it was the most important philosophic piece I had ever read.

So in 1933, when I started writing *Nine Chains to the Moon*, I asked his publishers whether I could quote from that piece, and they gave me permission to do it. I started the book with a chapter called "Tentative Cosmic Inventory," in which I entered everything humanity knew at the time—the limits of what science had been able to find. This led me to think about Einstein.

You see, I was convinced that Einstein's relativity, deriving from the measurements of the speed of light would
"catalyze a chain reaction ultimately altering altogether the patterning of man's everyday world."

Then I wrote a chapter in which I said that I could see how a man like that came to formulate his equation. A man with a philosophy like that, who worked in the Swiss patent office for a number of years ... If you know anything about patents, when you're writing your claim you have a piece that reviews the state of the art at that time and why what you've invented is an invention—a breakthrough. In Switzerland, the most prominent of all manufacturing and scientific inventions were clocks; and Einstein would then come to one patent after another about timekeeping devices. Each would make clear that there had never been any exact timekeepers and describe why this one might make it more accurate.

This made him realize that there was no such thing as exact time. Newton had assumed an absolutely exact time permeating all of universe uniformly. I'm sure this got him to thinking about the phenomenon of time and how and why Newton was wrong. This is typical of the way I reasoned.

I then wrote out my interpretation of how Einstein arrived at what he did, everything leading from his cosmic viewpoint and what I knew about his life. So there's two chapters: one on his philosophy and the other on how he came onto it. Then I said that whenever a great scientist makes an original breakthrough, he has to wait a long time before the academy agrees. It takes much longer before it gets into the schoolbooks and begins to affect the kids, and so forth. Then, finally, people begin to invent in terms of, "This is the way the world really is," and some industry produces something that begins to affect the home environment.

So I wrote a third chapter, "$E=MC^2=$ Mrs. Murphy's Horsepower," about what life would be like for Mrs. Murphy if Einstein were proven to be correct. At the time I was writing this, of course, it hadn't been proven yet. So there were these three chapters in the book on Einstein...

The only reason I got it published was that Chris Morley was such a friend of mine.

He told Frank Henry that he ought to publish my book, and Frank did whatever Chris told him. He was devoted to Chris and felt obligated to him for moving all his books. And so they were going ahead with it. But then it got into the hands of one of the editors who wrote me that he had found three chapters on Einstein; that at that time there were supposed to be only ten people in the world who understood Einstein and that "I looked up the list and you're not on it. I think we'd be a party to charlatanry if we were to publish it."

The publishers said who was I
—I wasn't one of those handful of legendary scientists who alone could understand Einstein—
who was I to link the great man with Mrs. Murphy?

So I rashly wrote back and said that Dr. Einstein has come to America, he's in Princeton. Why don't you send him my typescript? But it never occurred to me that Lippincott would do that.

About six months later I got a telephone call from a Doctor Fishbein who lived on Riverside Drive in New York, and he said, "My friend Dr. Albert Einstein is coming in this weekend to stay with me and he has your text with him and he'd like to talk to you about it. Would you be free on Sunday night?" And so of course I said, I wouldn't let anything get in the way, and I went to this apartment house.

It was a big apartment this man had; a very large living room, like a ballroom, and Dr. Einstein was sitting up at the head with a huddle of people around him. I was really extraordinarily moved. He really seemed to have an aura, almost a mystical aura, about him. As soon as I was introduced he got up and took me to the library. There on the desk my text was sitting.

He sat down in front of it and I sat on the other side of the desk. He said he had read my typescript and he approved of my explanation of how he had arrived at his conclusions and was going to notify my publishers to that effect. "But," he then said, "young man, this chapter on Mrs. Murphy—you amaze me. I cannot myself conceive of anything I have done ever having the slightest practical application." And here I had all this practical application! At any rate, he did notify Lippincott and they did go ahead.

Near the end of 1938 Otto Hahn in Germany discovered neutron-induced fission of uranium. Hahn, Germany's outstanding radiochemist, worked since 1907 with Lise Meitner, who was the physicist of the group until she was forced to leave by the Nazis in 1938. He notified her of the discovery in Denmark where she was working with Niels Bohr.

Then, when Bohr came to the United States, he discussed the splitting of the uranium atom with Einstein and other American scientists. Some tests were run at Columbia University and they saw that Hahn and Strassman were absolutely right.

Chris Morley

They knew that President Roosevelt wouldn't be interested in any other scientist but Einstein; that no one else would have enough credit so that if he said, "This is really atomic energy," 'cause there'd never been any such thing in the world, he'd be the only one Franklin Roosevelt would believe. So Einstein did that; and all that's quite well known. I have a copy of the letter written by Einstein to Roosevelt—it's on my desk in Philadelphia.

I'm the only person that heard Einstein say that extraordinary thing—and what he must have felt then! Oh, he also said the only reason he did what he did was that he hoped it would be of use to cosmologists—people that were thinking of the universe in a very big way—he didn't think it would have any practical application. His equation was certainly proven right with the atomic pile and Fermi in Chicago. Then think of its first practical application being Hiroshima, and that really the rest of his life was absolutely blighted.

You remember that poem I wrote in the 60's for *Saturday Review*?
  Fission verified Einstein's hypothesis:
  Change is normal;
  Thank you, Albert!

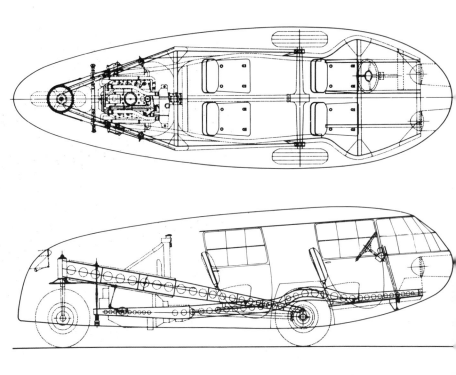

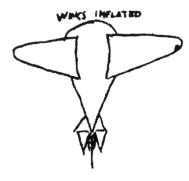

More and more people were beginning to get excited about my Dymaxion House. My idea had been air-deliverability of the house with all its autonomous equipment—the whole thing weighing only three tons—to be installed in very remote places without highways or runways for airplanes. You could set down the Dymaxion House like a bird landing on a rock someplace, and it could be anchored by cables to keep it from blowing over.

o I turned my attention to transport, to developing a vehicle that would
ke you back and forth from these remote places. And I wanted it to fly the
ay a duck flies: a duck doesn't soar like a seagull can; it has to flap its
ings very rapidly and has jets under each of its wings. The jets give it a little
evation; then, due to shape and elevation, it falls in its preferred direction;
o it plummets. It lifts and plummets; lifts and plummets.

wanted to develop such a flying machine:
ou'd simply get your elevation and plummet forward,
nd when you wanted to stop,
ou'd stop yourself just the way the duck does.
wanted an omnimedium, wingless transport
hat would go on the ground, in the water, and in the air,
vith angularly orientable twin-jet stilts.
ut there weren't any jets at the time,
ny more than there were helicopters that could air-deliver the Dymaxion
louse itself.

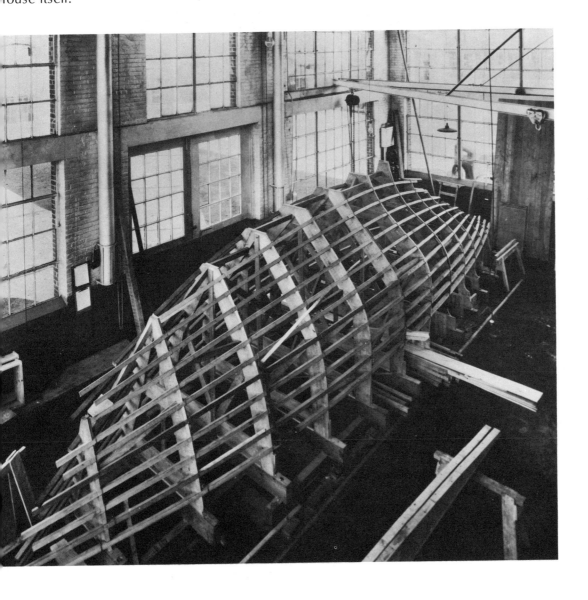

So in 1933, with the little money I had from lecturing and from *Shelter* magazine in cash in my pocket, I went to Bridgeport, Connecticut, where I rented a little factory to explore and develop the ground-taxiing qualities of such a Dymaxion transport. Noguchi made the plaster models under my instruction.

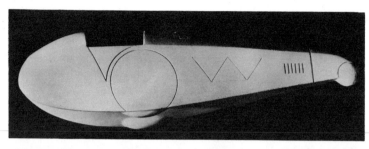

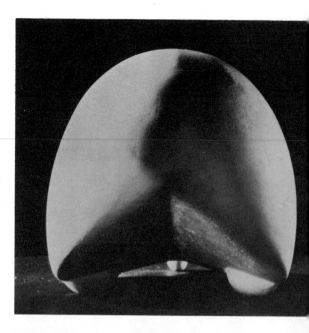

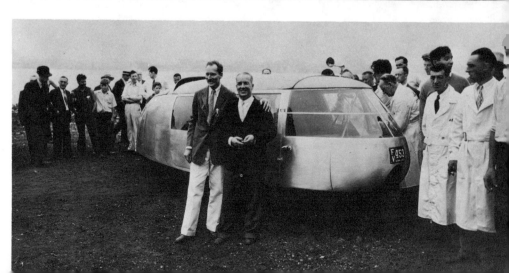

I was lucky to get Starling Burgess as my chief engineer, one of the world's finest airplane designers and leading designer of racing yachts. He had to complete a design for a new yacht, so we made a deal: I helped him with that and he helped me produce the first of the Dymaxion transports.

It had a streamlined belly, front-wheel traction,
driving the wheels on the ground just near where the jets would come out when it was in the air;
and it steered with a third wheel at its tail,
the way a fish or bird or a boat or airplane must steer.

A front-steered car with the king pins could only steer up to a 34-degree angle, whereas I could turn my rudder post so I could give it 90-degrees rudder if I wanted to. I could even reverse myself, make a 180-degree turn, hooking the inboard front wheel on the turn, making it circle on only one foot. No motorcycle or anything like it can do that.

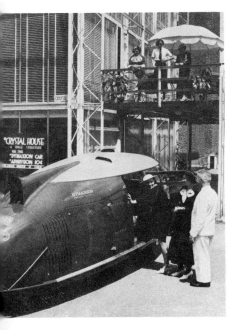

It was so extraordinarily stable. The center of gravity was very, very low. It was the first vehicle that ever had its center of gravity brought forward to the midpoint of the wheelbase.

Henry Ford had given me a 70 percent discount on all the equipment I could use, and with his then brand-new V-8 engine, we finally got the 90 horsepower engine to do 120 mph.

I made two more cars after that, three in all, between '33 and '35—all with three wheels, rear engines and streamlined.

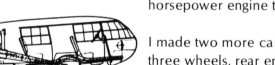

It proved to be a very good vehicle, with very high efficiency, seating eleven passengers and averaging 22 miles to the gallon; sometimes I got as much as 30 miles. And because it was steered from the rear, when I wanted to park in a space just the length of my car, I would simply bring my nose into the curb and throw my rear wheels sideways, and she went right in—flop—like that.

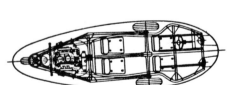

I knew people would call it an automobile,
but it wasn't designed to be just an automobile.
It was designed, as I said, to become an omnimedium,
wingless, flying device
with angularly orientable twin-jet stilts—
like the jets coming out from beneath the wings of a duck.

It was when I had my Dymaxion car that I met Frank Morley, who was in the publishing business and had a house here and in England, and his brothers, Chris and Felix; all three were Rhodes scholars. I became part of the Three-Hours-for-Lunch Club that Chris and Don Marquis had started. Don was the author of *archy and mehitabel*.

Frank came over from England with his friend, E. V. Lucas of *Punch*. E. V. Lucas wanted to see my Dymaxion car which he'd heard about, so I took him out for rides. He loved it. Then Frank came over with H. G. Wells and Wells wanted to ride in the car; so we did.

And I drove both of those men all over greater New York, coming up, say, on Fifth Avenue—with a policeman on every corner. At any rate, whenever we were stopped people immediately ran from both curbs and surrounded the car. She drew incredible crowds.

The same thing happened when we went down to Wall Street. We got there at noontime, and the crowd filled up the streets to such an extent that the police wouldn't let me go below Canal Street after that. They said we can't have these unhandlable crowds! And whenever I'd get out of the car, leave it at the curb, and come out again—and nobody knew who I was—they wouldn't let me get into my own car and resented my taking it away.

Top: Passengers—
Left, Amelia Earhart
seated inside, and
H.G. Wells, properly
hatted for a drive
in my Dymaxion
"Car." Below: Chris
and I toast the
Three-Hours-for-
Lunch Club.

At any rate, Wells was riding around New York with me and the windows were just plastered with faces looking in. Nobody recognized him at all; in England he was used to being recognized and he'd say, "It's quite amazing t find myself here and nobody pays the slightest bit of attention to you or me They act as if it's their car, as if the car belongs to them."

On account of that, the cars in his *The Shape of Things to Come* were very much like the Dymaxion car.

Wells was staying at one of the fancy men's clubs—I think it was the Brook Club—and he asked me up there. By this time, d'ye see, I'd been drinking again, and I'm having drinks at the Brook Club and he's saying, in his British accent, "I don't like to boast, y'know, but I subscribe to *Fortune* magazine, and I read about your Dymaxion House this spring in an article by Archibal MacLeish. So I'm very familiar with your work."

All this opened up my adventures with Chris Morley and the Three-Hours-for-Lunch Club with Don Marquis and so many other really wonderful people who were members of the club.

Chris wrote a book dedicated to me called *Streamlines* that has the car as the main feature. His dedication in that is one of the nicest things ever written about me.

"For Buckminster Fuller, scientific idealist,
whose innovations proceed not just from technical dexterity,
but from an organic vision of life."

Chris Morley, center, is wearing a laurel wreath. I am to the far left — at the Gotham Book Mart.

In 1936 I was asked to go into research at Phelps Dodge, the third largest copper company in the world. They wanted to know what I saw as the future of the copper industry. I had access to the great world copper cartel. For the first time, I was able to go around and gather information from big international corporations and enlarge my inventory of resources which I now named, Inventory of World Resources, Human Trends, and Human Needs.

They also gave me the chance to make a prototype of my Dymaxion bathroom. In 1930 I had developed a full-size model of a bathroom-kitchen, back to back, for my Dymaxion House where I manifolded their plumbing hook-up—a method used today in almost all housing developments. In those days, I had not only been amazed at the crudeness of the building technology which was at exactly the opposite pole from that being put into weaponry, but I was also shocked to discover that no scientist had ever looked at the plumbing.

The Dymaxion bathroom is the solution to the place we all go to bathe and to wash and to take care of the human processes. I was able to do a whole bathroom, including what we call manifold plumbing, all reassembled and everything, the manifold of wiring and the manifold of air conditioning— and it all weighed only 450 pounds.

Below: Left, Dymaxion bathroom, die-stamped in one piece. Right, patent drawing.

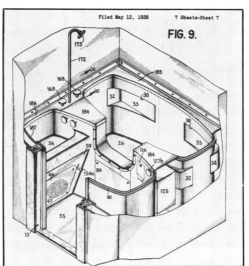

Filed May 12, 1938   7 Sheets-Sheet 7

FIG. 9.

As usual, in 1972 a community leader told me there was a new industry coming to his city, "Mass-produced bathrooms!" I said, "They're right on time—I designed the first one forty-five years ago."

From Phelps Dodge I went over to *Fortune* magazine as science and technology consultant; and for the magazine's tenth anniversary in 1940, I persuaded them to do a study of the world's total resources. That issue went into three printings, and I was able to bring it and my information up to date.

In the summer of 1940, Chris Morley and I were driving through Missouri—Hannibal, Missouri, where Mark Twain lived—and I noticed in the wheat fields, a row of glistening, galvanized, corrugated-steel grain bins. I told Chris that there was the most efficient engineering unit for a small prefabricated house now on inventory in mass-production industry.

"That grain bin would provide enough room to house a small family at a cost of less than $1 per square foot of floor space with fireproof construction," I said, "and that's 80 percent below construction costs in the building industry. Those bins could easily be converted to dwelling machines." But I was broke of course, and couldn't do anything about it.

Soon afterward *Kitty Foyle* became a great success and Chris said, "Bucky, Kitty wants you to go out and see the Butler grain-bin people, and get that thing going." So I whipped out the basic plans for the Dymaxion Deployment Unit and took them on a flyer to Kansas City with Chris putting up the money for the trip. But he put up something no money can buy—a backing of creative enthusiasm, a confidence and joy in individual initiative, amusement over the paradoxes of adversity, and complete submission to what Chris spoke of at Don Marquis's funeral as "the Holiest Ghost we shall ever know: creative imagination."

The converted bins were an instant success: the Army Signal Corps and Air Corps were able to have the first radar operating huts, light enough to be flown and simple enough to be speedily assembled, in very remote places. Hundreds saw service in the Pacific Islands during the war; hundreds were pirated by the Saudi Arabians for use in the Persian Gulf. The Museum of Modern Art set up one unit as a special exhibit in its garden; and I donated one unit to Bennington College. I think years after, Louis Horst, Martha Graham's mentor and music adviser lived in it. At any rate, with the wartime restriction on the use of steel, the supply officials decided that the unit, used only as a dwelling, was of low priority.

In the end, it was there, at the Butler Company in Kansas City, that I decided to quit drinking. By this time...I was, older...It was 1940–41. World War II was coming on. Charles Edison, Edison's son, was Secretary of the Navy, and he liked me very much and asked me to come down and talk to all the admirals about my inventions.

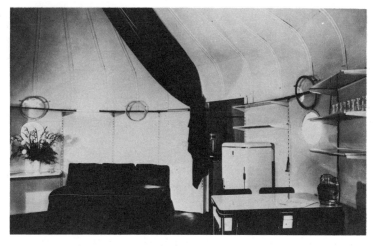

I found that when I talked about an invention and I had been drinking, they'd
say, "This guy is plastered." I found that in order to gain credibility I would
have to give up drinking. So, chop! And it really was a great relief.

Then I was appointed head of mechanical engineering on the Board of Economic Warfare. I was responsible for studying all world economic resources. Once again I was able to enlarge my resource data enormously.

I just want you to realize that the kind of resource information I have isn't duplicated anywhere—not in the Kremlin or the White House or the Pentagon—I'm very confident of that.

It wasn't until 1944 that I was able to develop the first actual Dymaxion House with the Beech Aircraft Company in Wichita, Kansas. You see, late in the war the aircraft industry was in great trouble due to labor shortages: the workers did not feel that there was any post-war future for the industry after the war, and began quitting their jobs to go to some other job during the war that would have a better future.

Then some labor officials, such as Walter Reuther of the U.A.W. and Harvey Brown, president of the International Association of Machinists, the War Manpower Commission, etc., remembered that I had developed the Dymaxion House which could be produced in the aircraft industry—that, in fact, could only be produced there. They asked me about it.

I said it could do two things: provide an immediate solution to the looming postwar housing shortage, and it might provide permanent employment in the aircraft field—because there is no basic difference between the fabricating of aluminum parts for the Dymaxion House and for the fuselages of the most advanced B-29 aircraft.

They arranged a meeting for me with Beech Aircraft in Wichita, Kansas; and it was agreed that I could come in, have access to the tools and top engineers and mechanics in a going aircraft plant on a cost basis, without any capital investment.

So I resigned my government post and moved to Wichita.
And I began to develop drawings and specifications for the new Dymaxion
dwelling machine.
We did produce it—between 1944 and '46—
after going through some progressive prototypes,
cleaning up many of my thoughts over the years since 1927,
before it was finally shown to the public.
It wasn't built by hand
but on production machinery at the aircraft plant,
and with the aircraft industry's extraordinary structural capabilities,
of aircraft materials with aircraft tools.
Anyone visiting the plant, wouldn't be able to tell the difference
between the airplane parts and the parts being made for the house.
It was made of aircraft aluminum, except for the mast itself,
which was made of stainless steel, 22 feet high.

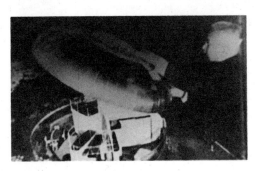

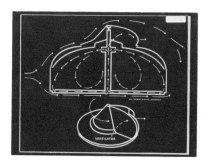

On top is a huge ventilator, 18 feet in diameter,
which rotates like a wind-T at an airport.
A low pressure would form at this point,
where we then had the ventilator tail open.
That pulled the air of the house through—
so it was completely air-conditioned.

This house was made of aluminum, stainless steel, and plastics
instead of bricks and lumber;
it hangs rather than sits;
it's more or less circular instead of square,
giving maximum strength for each pound of material used.

It was made so it could be installed wherever you want it,
so that you could call up and say,
"I'd like my dwelling machine here," or "over there,"
like any service industry.

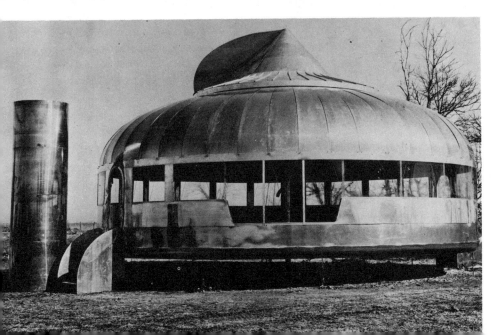

Board Chairman
Fuller

Bucky with Marian
Anderson testing
the acoustics
of Dymaxion
House.

was during the war that I was being asked to give talks—by the Boeing Company and other companies and institutions—and I came East. We were living in Forest Hills in New York then, and I was asked to speak at the Institute of Design in Chicago.

They were crazy about my presentation and apparently as a consequence I got a call from Joseph Albers at Black Mountain College, to be one of their summer professors for the summer of 1948, and I accepted.

It was at Black Mountain that I met John Cage and Merce Cunningham, who were there, Bill de Kooning and his wife Elaine, Arthur Penn, the Alberses, of course, Ruth Asawa, Albert Lanier, who later married Ruth, and Ken Nelson.

That group decided they wanted to put on a play and they wanted me to be in it. And I said, "I can't act; I never have. All I can do is talk spontaneously, but I can't do anything where you have to rehearse."

And they said, "You must try. You're going to be the star of this thing, *The Ruse of Medusa* by Erik Satie—and you're going to be the Medusa."

Bucky with Merce Cunningham in *The Ruse of the Medusa*

Well, I was working very hard on my new mathematics at that time, spendi[ng] hours and hours in my room and not eating lunch, and when they said, "You've got to do it," I said, "Well, maybe...." I was trying very, very hard [to] discipline myself and I thought this would be another kind of discipline, to make myself behave in ways I'd never done before.
So I finally agreed to do it.

I found it very difficult to remember the lines and we would have rehearsa[l] after rehearsal. At any rate I did learn them. Then Arthur Penn showed up and he became director of the production.

I'm up on the stage and he would take positions all around the theater where the audience would be, and he'd keep at me about speaking up and speaking up and speaking up—he was marvelous at it. I'm sure it's affected my whole stage presence. Today I really know whether I'm getting across t[o] those people in the back of the hall.

Bucky with Elaine de Kooning and Bill Shrager

In his strange way John Cage thought it would be one of the funniest things to get me on the stage—you know how he laughs about things—and it would amuse him tremendously because it would seem so unlike me, dancing, singing, rhyming. Of course Medusa didn't do those things until I did it. I made a completely new Medusa, I have to tell you that.

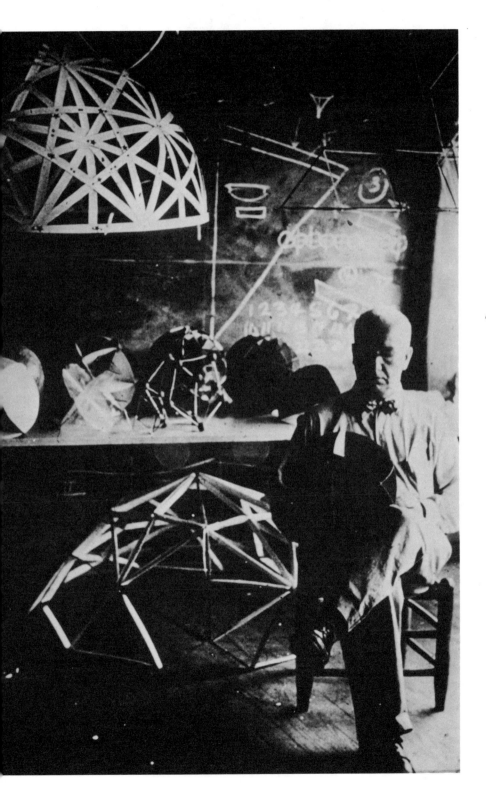

Bucky and his models at Black Mountain

With Ruth Asawa

"What Albers did graphically," Ruth Asawa pointed out, *"Bucky did by trial and error, just by putting marbles and pieces of paper together. He used to unload his little aluminum trailer and all these models and structures came bouncing out. The idea he expressed to the college was that 'I am the most successful failure.'*

He gathered all this information and invention out of his experience. What impressed me most about both Bucky and Albers was that they made lifetime commitments: they weren't interested in ideas that were already solved; they were only interested in ideas that didn't have a shape yet."

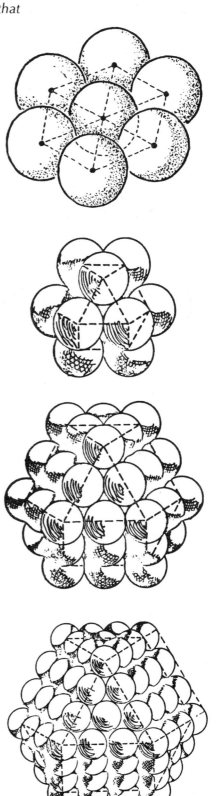

One of the important developments to grow out of Bucky's theories was the discovery by his student and later well-known sculptor Kenneth Snelson, of tension integrity.

The tensegrity mast demonstrates the use of tension and compression within the same structure.
Aluminum tubes, for example, are the compressive forces and are separated by thin metal wires which are all in tension.
The continuous pull of the wires is resisted by the discontinuous tubes—
discontinuous compression/continuous tension—
illustrating tensional integrity, or tensegrity.
Structures built according to tensegrity theory become stronger as their size increases and could, theoretically, cover limitless areas
—even the entire earth.

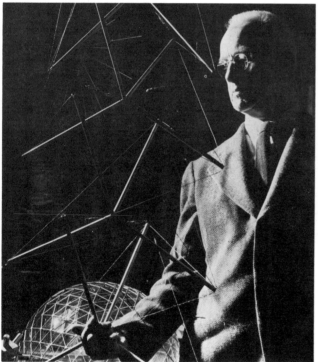

he octet truss was composed of alternating tetrahedrons and octohedrons
hich dispersed load pressures equally along three sets of parallel planes.
ressure at any one point was immediately distributed
rough the entire structure,
ving it great strength while maintaining an impression
f laciness and delicacy in relation to its size.

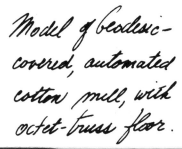

*Model of geodesic-
covered, automated
cotton mill, with
octet-truss floor.*

model - '52

hen the time came to use the octet truss in actual construction,
ucky was well prepared and successfully
ilt the Ford Rotunda — dome.

The Fifties:

Bucky and Anne are back in New York in a small cram-packed apartment in Forest Hills. Picture him then engulfed by his models and charts, the cosmic explorer rationalizing and writing his energetic-synergetic geometry and doodling his great circles, from both of which his domes will spring. (Allegra is away at Bennington College, pursuing her interest in the dance.)

From this modest base he sallies forth in accelerating acceleration to lecture, consult, design.
He's gone from "track to trackless, wire to wireless," if not to ephemeralization. The very model of a "comprehensive anticipatory design scientist," he spirals through wish-thought-deed, exploring the macro-meso-microcosm as natural philosopher, socioeconomist, and inventor of artifacts, especially of ever-bolder controlled environments. He lives totally in the process of the moment, the moment-becoming-future. Rarely does he find time to talk about the past; that was yesterday.

In 1951 Bucky's daughter, "laughing Allegra," and I are married.
This past Christmas, we were sitting around with family and a few friends, and I mentioned that I was starting to work on a picture-book biography of him. In the course of the conversation, Bucky formal-sounding, addressed the group:
"I want to tell you about a young man named Robert Snyder. He came to see my wife, Anne, in our little apartment back in 1950 to talk about marrying our daughter, Allegra. And it seems he was very dubious about me. He said, "Mr. Fuller was not a man of any substance." Anne told me about it; she felt she had to defend me against his onslaught." *(Laughter.)*

But, Bucky I protested, it was simply self-defense: I said that my family wouldn't regard you as any more substantial than Anne said her family regarded me." (Laughter.)

Are you going to include in your picture book the photo of yourself and Allegra at Bennington, the wedding picture with the wine glasses?
But, Bucky, I shouldn't include that—
My daughter getting married?
—unless you're in it; after all, the book's about you.
I'm not in it because I was taking the picture; and that seems to me to make it valid. For that matter, the picture I took of Allegra and you skating on the pond that Christmas in Newburyport, after we swept the little pond clean, d'ya remember that? I think—
How could I forget, Bucky; but the book is about you, not your photography.
—that ought to go in, too.

Allegra and Bob (Snyder) on their wedding day; and sending their Christmas greetings.

Filming him meant film-recording his work, metaphysical and physical. But he wouldn't sit still: more and more, it seemed to me an exercise in "Go and catch a falling star."

We must now run alongside him, pausing when possible for breath and notin
the highlights of his closely packed days, whether of snatches of his
metaphysical thinking aloud or glimpses of the physical artifacts, even bits of
autobiographical monologue that all too few moments permit. It would
perhaps be more appropriate to his life-style, to continue at this juncture
in the form of a journal and photo scrapbook.

However, Lord be thanked, there were moments:
throughout the years, Bucky has managed to take a few weeks during the
summer to return to his source, Bear Island, where he recharges his
batteries and, as he says, regenerates himself. He walks, talks, reflects…

does the housekeeping chores,

ows and sails,

skips stones,
studies them and other forms
in his most cherished "laboratory in nature."
Here, too, he does much of his exploratory "thinking aloud."

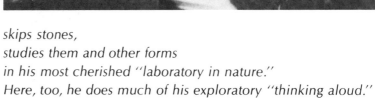

"Look at all the seals there..."

ook at all the seals there on Bear Island ledge sunning themselves. They
ook like a whole lot of rocks, but those are all seals. Lot of cormorants
ehind them, long-neckers....

Synergy

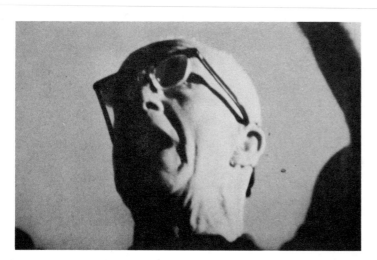

In order to be able to understand the great complexity of life and to understand what the universe is doing, the first word to learn is synergy. Synergy is the behavior of whole systems, unpredicted by the behavior of their parts. The most extraordinary example of it is what we call mass attraction. One great massive sphere and another massive sphere hung by tension members are attracted to one another. We find there is nothing in one sphere, in its own right, that predicts that it's going to be attracted to another. You have to have the two. It is, then, synergy which holds our earth together with the moon; and it is synergy which holds our whole universe together.

Synergy is the companion word to the word energy. Synergy means behavior of whole systems unpredicted by the behavior of any of the parts. It is the only word that means it. The fact that we are unfamiliar with the word means that we do not think there are behaviors of wholes unpredicted by parts.

Synergy is to energy as integration is to differentiation. Energy studies separate out—isolating phenomena out of total nature and total universe, and studying those separate phenomena. Synergy is associated behavior of the whole: great complexes all the way to total universe itself.

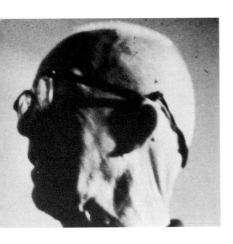

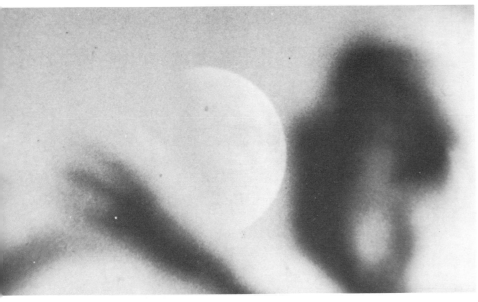

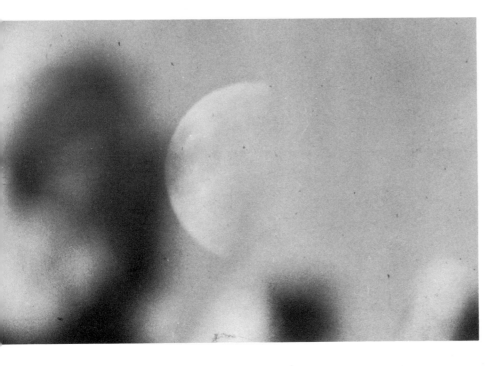

The speed of light had not been measured until we came into this century; no one had even supposed that light had a speed.

Therefore, all of the scientists before our century, looking at the stars, assumed that every star was always right there—that there was what we call "instant universe"—a complete misapprehension, because instant universe is in a sense a static thing. This idea derives from Newton's law that "at rest" was the norm; motion was abnormal.

Einstein paid great attention to Michelson-Morley's experiments that light does have speed, that it takes 8 minutes for light to get to us from the sun; it takes light 2½ years to get to us from the next nearest star;

looking at one star out here at night — it's a live show taking place 30,000 years ago. Light is just getting here this second. Right next to it is this star, a live show 3,000 years ago. Some of those stars are not even there anymore.

Einstein said quite clearly that our universe is an aggregate of nonsimultaneous and only partially overlapping energy-transformation events. Each one of these events is constantly transforming. Universe is, as Einstein said, a scenario; as for instance, a man is born, then he gets to be a father; he has children and grandchildren and then he dies. And they go on. But looking at the sky here, we are still seeing grandfather.

Universe is a scenario.
It's just in this century that we think so,
and society is not yet thinking in this way.
No single picture is going to tell you
that a caterpillar is going to become a butterfly;
and one picture won't tell you that a butterfly flies.

I don't think—as scientists had been thinking until then—that the energies of universe are always running down. I think that when energies leave the local system, they are taken on by another system.

Scientific review of experiments showed that that was exactly what was going on. So only in this century have we come to discover that energies are not lost, the universe is not running down, and our new norm is Einstein's norm that says energies are always transforming at the very highest velocities at which things can transform or change. The rate at which energy goes right away from itself radiantly is at the speed of light. So 186,000 miles per second is normal.

Anything we call "matter" is where energies trip themselves up like knots, develop local constrictions, and become matter—energy going around at the same rate, but locally.

The behavior of wholes, unpredicted by the behavior of its parts, can best be illustrated, I think, by chrome-nickel-steel—chromium, nickel, iron. The most important characteristic of strength of a material is its ability to stay in one piece when it's pulled— its tensile strength, in terms of its strength per square inch, PSI. The commercially available strength of iron at the very highest level is approximately 60,000 pounds per square inch; of chromium, about 70,000; and of nickel, about 80,000. The weakest is the iron.

We all know the saying
that a chain is only as strong
as its weakest link.

Well, experiment on chrome-nickel-steel, pull it apart, and you'll find that it is very much stronger than its weakest link of 60,000. In fact, it's much stronger than the 80,000, or its strongest link.
Thus the saying that a chain is as strong as its weakest link doesn't hold. So, let me say something that really seems very silly: Maybe a chain is as strong as the sum of the strength of all its links. Let's add up the 60,000 for the iron and the 70,000 for the chromium—that makes 130,000 pounds per square inch—then add the 80,000 for the nickel; that gives you 210,000. Then add the minor constituents of carbon and manganese—about 40,000—210,000 plus 40,000 = 250,000 pounds per square inch tensile strength.
Now the fact is that under testing, chrome-nickel-steel shows 350,000— or 100,000 pounds to the square inch, stronger than the combined strength of all the links.
This is typical synergy, and it is the synergy of the various alloy metals that have made industry able to do all kinds of things that man never knew he could do when he just did things statistically.

All economists work in terms of statistics, and all economists work in terms of the weakest link. So society's been utterly surprised by the continual abilities of technology to do more than they'd ever expected it could do: there's your synergy.

Synergy, the behavior of wholes unpredicted by the behavior of its parts, has a corollary to it: that with the known behavior of the whole and the known behavior of some of the parts, you will be able to find out about the other parts. Now, that's very interesting.

As for instance, we have the synergetic strategy of the Greeks, with their triangle.
They knew that the sums of the angles would always be 180 degrees.
So, knowing two sides and an angle, or two angles and a side, you could find out about the three other parts—because there are six parts to a triangle: three sides and three angles. This synergetic capability was used by astronomers when Isaac Newton developed his theory of gravitation.

"Gravitation," his opponents said, "pulls these great masses. Well, we can't explain the solar system and the planets unless, one, Newton was wrong or, two, there are other planets, very large ones, much bigger than we've ever seen before. It's most unlikely that they're there, so probably Newton was wrong."

But, in due course, the two planets that had to be there were found to be there—Pluto and Uranus. And they were just the right size and in the right position.

This was typical of synergetic prediction: The known behavior of the whole required the behavior of the other two parts. This is fundamental to the most powerful parts of science, yet it's not used at all in our educational system. We go precisely in the opposite way, starting off our children with parts, an A, a B, a C; then we put those together—
and nobody knows about synergy.
I find that society is just groping around with parts, never understanding wholes and continually being surprised by them.

When we deal with systems—and systems are conceptual and subdivide the total universe into outsideness and insideness—systems return upon themselves in a plurality of directions, whether they're spheres or cubes or crocodiles. The universe itself is a system, and it is a quality of a system that it has unit surface.

Frequently, he is obliged to yield to requests for "thinking aloud" publicly, especially when they come from down-East neighbors.

I was asked by the Unitarian Church at Sunset, just across the Bay, at the tip of Deer Isle, to give a talk. Bob called it a sermon; he said I was following in the tradition of my preacher forebears.

This is such an extraordinarily beautiful day. All of us who love Maine think of Maine in this way—that we love our fog too. The beauty of today makes me feel very powerfully that nature is trying to tell us—that God is trying to tell all of us—that our world can be beautiful, that it can really work. What we ought to be doing is making it possible for humanity, not only to survive on our earth, but to enjoy the kind of beauty that today tries to tell us we can enjoy...

Throughout man's history, the average man in his average lifetime has seen only a millionth of the surface of our globe. That's a very tiny amount, and it's not surprising that he thinks about the earth in a way that is really not correct at all. His senses are focused on a seemingly vast expanse that goes on and on. It is important for us to remind ourselves as quickly as we can how many misconceptions we are all still operating under.

I'm sure everyone in this room uses the words up and down. If anybody does not use the words up and down, will you please raise your hand? (I have to be careful not to say, "Put up your hand.") The words up and down were invented by man to accommodate his experience of seeing only a millionth of the earth's surface, because the world seems to go on and on beyond his personal experience. In the desert or out on the deep sea, it seems to go off into infinity.

The temples of Cambodia are built symbolically to represent a model of what the people thought the world was. They rise out of a moat or lake, and in the center of this little island, the temple goes up into great pinnacles, like formalized mountains. The farther into the center you go, the higher the pinnacles of the temple rise; as, going into the interior of the land, the farther you go, the surer you are to come to mountains. Around the temple-island there is a carving that ends in great serpent heads, representing Naga, the giant sea serpent that surrounds the entire island.

I'm sure most of us are still using expressions that come from the time of those islands. Many of us speak of the four corners of the earth. That's the very model of a flat earth with corners pointed in specific directions. And if the earth is flat, all the perpendiculars to the earth must be parallel to one another—that's very simple, isn't it? Therefore, they all go this way or that way; and this is called "up," and this, "down." And inasmuch as you see parallel lines going away from you like railroad tracks converging, you sort of say that they intend to converge into heaven and they tend to converge into hell.

Now once you discover that your earth is a sphere, you find that none of the perpendiculars are parallel to each other. Each is absolutely, completely independent. Thus no part of the universe can be designated as "up" or "down."

Fliers, when they began to go around the earth very quickly, became aware of the fact that in terms of the way they used to speak they were upside down, and since they didn't feel upside down, they invented "come in for a landing," and "go out." So the right words to use are, "come in" toward various masses in the universe or the planet, and "go out from" the moon or Mars. So in the next few weeks, if you'll just say to yourselves, "I'm going outstairs" and "I'm going instairs," you'll also begin to ask yourselves, "What is it I'm going in towards?" You are going in towards the center of our planet. And you will gradually begin to realize that you are really on board a spaceship—a great, spherical spaceship.

You'll find you're coddling yourselves and you're very easy on yourselves in dealing with these errors you've been making. But when you begin to do a little housecleaning in terms of what you've found out, you begin to think in some new ways...

We start off by teaching our children to give up the reality of feeling themselves in the round and try to get them to pretend to be on a flat plane. Theoretically, we couldn't be more anxious to help these children not be at the disadvantage we experienced. But when we teach our children geometry, we start off by dealing with a plane going to infinity and lines that go to infinity.

That's an annoying kind of thought for a young person, for someone suddenly to give him infinity, something he can't possibly comprehend or resolve because it is incomprehensible. So it's really quite an unfriendly thing to say, "Here's something nice and simple, darling; it's a line that goes on to infinity. Later on," we say, "we'll get to solid geometry."

All this is extraordinarily difficult; and one reason very exceptional children do not do well in mathematics is because you ask them to do some very preposterous things. We'll just have to remind ourselves that no one—no scientist, no physicist, no genealogist, no physiologist—has ever discovered anything that can be called a solid. What they have discovered is that our physical universe is energy, and that energy events are relatively very, very remote from one another: atoms, the proton, and electron are as remote from each other as our sun and earth. Physics has found no solids! So to keep on teaching our children the word solid immediately is to drive home a way of thinking that is going to be neither reliable nor useful.

There are no surfaces, there are no solids, there are no straight lines, there are no planes.

Once you begin to catch on that you're aboard a spaceship, you begin to get an inkling of what a fantastic design this all is. I would like to point out you that just a hundred years ago each human being was thought of as completely responsible and conscious, as long as he was awake. If he was drunk you'd say he wasn't quite as responsible; but a man who was neither drunk nor asleep was taken to be completely conscious of everything about him and therefore responsible for everything he did.

Just a short time ago historically, Sigmund Freud upset man's thinking by demonstrating that there were a great many things people did that were subconsciously coordinated and over which we really had no conscious control at all. That was just yesterday. Today, nuclear physicists have come to the realization that we are 99.999 percent subconsciously coordinated. Our brains have approximately a quadrillion times a quadrillion atoms operating in absolutely superb design coordination by which, for instance, you and I are communicating.

Just check up on yourselves.

I'm sure none of you know what you're doing with your supper. All you know is you've loaded it in, and you're not saying, "I'm going to send some of it off to this gland and some to that, and tomorrow morning I'm going to grow some hair." I'll simply assert all of you are almost completely automated and always have been. And you talk about automation as though it were something new and rather scary.

Our universe is an extraordinarily automated, fantastic piece of design. And in this design, here is our spaceship earth upon which human beings have been living for two million years without even knowing they've been aboard a ship—including yourselves. You're not thinking that way even now. But when you realize you are aboard this tiny ship, things are very different from the way they were thought about in the Roman Empire....
All the periods of history from which most of the philosophy comes and all our ways of looking at things that we have in our schoolbooks and universities, are eras when man thought of the earth as flat.
Julius Caesar, Genghis Khan—all of them—
thought the earth went on to infinity.
The Roman Empire was simply the known area, and it controlled the known area. Out beyond the areas of empires, you came to some very dangerous people, and beyond that, to dragons,
and beyond *that,* you'd better not go.
Now if the earth went to infinity, which they thought it did,
then there were an infinite number of chances that there could just be something out there that could take care of all our problems.
If we just would keep exploring a little more daringly,
we would come to the Great Roast Beef Mountain.

I'm convinced our troubles spring from continually feeling so sort of comfortable with, "Well, that's the way I learned it; that was good enough for me, and we did get along, and we did have a lot of fun, so let's leave it that way. It's too much trouble to rewrite books, we bought all those libraries, we taught all our teachers to teach that way"—so you just keep on teaching error...

A revised edition of the Dymaxion map was published. It grew out of his geometry: a geometric form such as "an icosahedron can be projected outwardly onto the surface of a sphere," or vice versa like unpeeling an orange and laying it out flat. It was the first map projection patented in the United States, and it was first published cut-out and fold-in, in Life *magazine (1943) as a "Dymaxion." The new edition was more accurately titled, "Air Ocean World Map."*

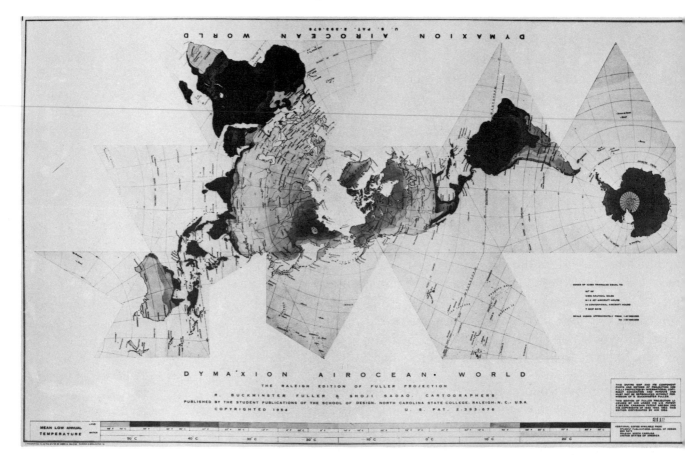

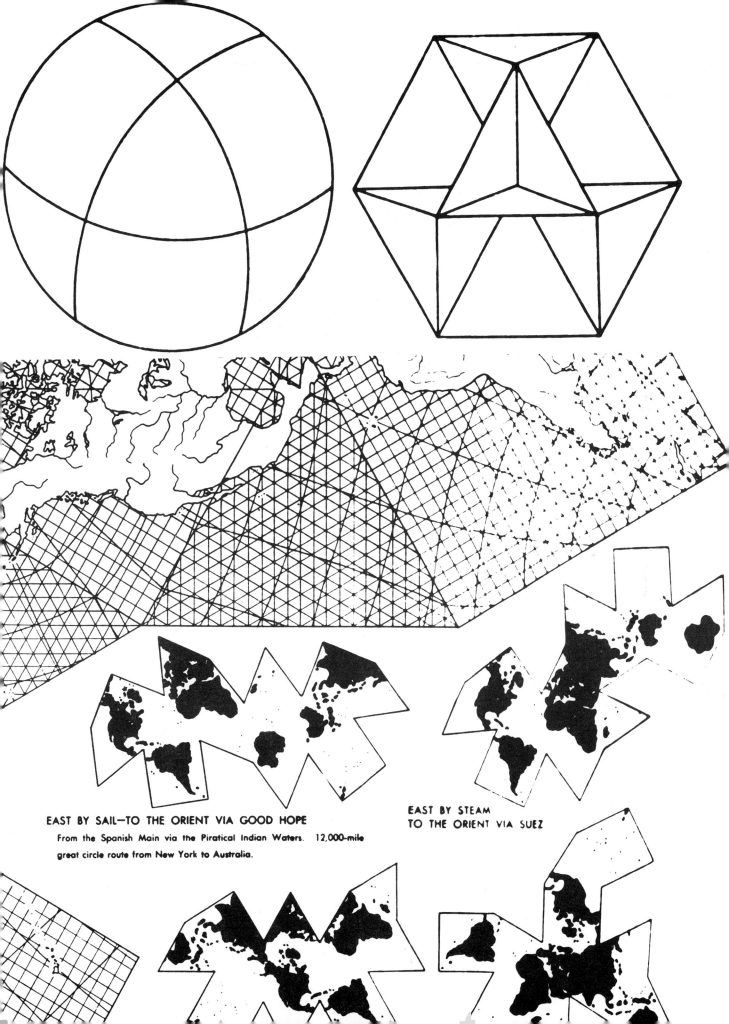

EAST BY SAIL—TO THE ORIENT VIA GOOD HOPE

From the Spanish Main via the Piratical Indian Waters. 12,000-mile great circle route from New York to Australia.

EAST BY STEAM
TO THE ORIENT VIA SUEZ

Geometry

Euler, the mathematician, made a very extraordinary contribution to humanity when he conceived and announced that all pattern of universe can be broken down into three clearly rememberable and differentiable aspects. He said look at any painting, any drawing, research your memory, you'll find everything breaks down into lines, areas, and crossings.

Mathematically you can describe all pattern phenomena, all conceptuality, all of thinking, by just what we call angles and frequencies.

Those lines of Euler's take some time to be generated.
How long they take to be generated is measured by cycles.
You look at your watch, you look at so many seconds:
there are so many cycles, so many heartbeats.
So you go in this direction on this line for so many heartbeats, so many seconds.
Then you change your direction.
Changing direction, you have to say,
"What is the angle of change?"

Now in order to start talking angle at all,
you have to have some line of reference.
The line of reference, say,
is between your head and your feet.
So there's that line, that axis.

So we find all phenomena in universe can be described mathematically by
angle and frequency change. Now that we know that time is measured
by cycles and lines are so many cycles long, we begin to think about patterns in a very mutable kind of way.

For example, here is a necklace,
and it is a necklace because I can drape it over my neck and shoulders.
It drapes because the angles are varying;
the lines are staying the same and aren't changing; what is changing are the
angles.

I'm going to take out one of the beads.
The necklace is still nice and flexible and still drapable.
I put my head through and it bends all over the place.
I'm going to take out one more, and it's still flexible—
with a vee in front and a vee in back.

You and I tend to call what we now have left, a square.
I can still put my head through it. When I was in school the teacher said
the basis of geometry is the square.
But the only reason it held its shape was because
the blackboard was holding its shape.
It had no integrity whatsoever.

A little child doesn't like that at all.
So he says I'm going to take one *more* out.
Suddenly, a very extraordinary thing happens—it's no longer flexible.
It won't change its shape!
Boy! I can put it over my head here, but it doesn't flex or drape.
This is what we call a tri-angle—three angles.
And the triangle is the only stable structure.

The angle won't change, and it was all in the angles.

So the triangle turns out to be structure.
It consists of six completely independent parts:
three of these flexible angles, and three of these push-pull compressions.
One pair of these sides work like levers;
the further they come out here, the more work they can do.

We come to the very ends of these levers,
and we put another push-pull member in here,
and it stabilizes the opposite angle.
So a triangle is a pattern
where each side stabilizes the opposite angle with minimum effort.

What we then call a structure in our universe is a complex of energy events
interacting to produce a stable pattern. The triangle is the only inter-self-
stabilizing set of events. Triangle is structure, structure is triangle. So when I
want to build something, and really make it work,
I've got to use all triangles.

Most people think of a building as cubical, and it hasn't any structural stability whatsoever. The angles are all unstable. The only reason they stand is that we put nails in the corners. So I've got to find a way whereby everything gains in stability. I'd like to make what they call a basic structure; and I'd like to make it into a system where I have an insideness and an outsideness.

I can't get something that has an insideness and an outsideness unless I have one more point. And that gives me the tetrahedron: *tetra* is four in Greek, so that gives us a 1-2-3-4-sided figure.

We'd like to find its relationship to the other basic structural systems.

When you take an action, for instance you step forward—you push the earth backward. Or a car starts up on a gravel path, it kicks the stones backward. Every action has reaction. Now not only does every action have a reaction, it also has a resultant.

Because we now know about the speed of light, we know there is a time lag between action and reaction and resultant. You jump off a boat and it takes little time for you to hit the other boat and you've pushed the boat you jumped off, pushed the boat you land on—so there's action, reaction, resultant. This is true of every experience, every event, in the universe.

Thus, every event in the universe has three parts: action, reaction, and resultant. These are energy events and we call them vectors. The vector depends on how much energy is being expended, what its mass is, in what direction it's going, and at what velocity.

All our experiences involve energy;
all the physical universe involves it.
These energies are operating at various directions.
A vector is an energy action in a specific direction, like a thrown spear.

There's some quantity of the energy as mass, and that energy action is going in some direction, so it has a velocity relative to all our other experiences. We then take the mass and multiply it by the velocity, and that gives us the length of the line of a vector. And it's going in a specific direction in relation to our other experiences. A vector has a specific angle, and direction, and specific length.

There are two fundamental kinds of energy events—proton and neutron. The proton has its energy side-effects; the proton has its electron and its anti-neutrino; and the neutron has its neutrino and its positron. And each one of those is called in physics one-half quantum, one-half of Planck's constant, one-half spin—any of those three.

Now, I'm going to put one half quantum together with another half quantum, and we find we must always put it together in an absolutely consistent way, joining the positive ends with the open angles—male goes to female. We put it together, and suddenly we come to our old friend, the tetrahedron, which has four triangles and six edges, or vectors, and one unit of quantum.

There are two other structural systems in the universe besides the tetrahedron. The octahedron with twelve edges, or vectors, and two units of quantum; and the icosahedron with thirty edges, or vectors, and five units of quantum.

So we now see a very important conceptuality beginning to characterize physics and all structural understanding. Remembering that a basic unit of quantum has six edges—or six vectors—a basic energy event has six vectors. If I use the volume of the tetrahedron as unity, this is the one that gives me the most volume with the least structure. It gives me the sharpest, the greatest strength, because these three legs, like any tripod, are much more vigorous in their support. If you begin to flatten out like that, like your own legs spreading out, it gets weaker and weaker.

The octahedron has four volumes, and here I get two units of quantum. The icosahedron has almost—pretty close to—twenty full volumes, I'm getting twenty units of volume for five units of quantum invested. So we get the most volume with the least quantum in the icosahedron. So that becomes the very basic structure in nature. I use it for geodesic domes, and nature uses it for all the protein shells of all the viruses.

The icosahedron is still very strong because it is triangular or basic structure. So this is the one that gives you the most volume, and I can fortify any one of those by putting a little local tetrahedron in there, to give it the greatest strength. That's the reason I make my goedesic structures that way.

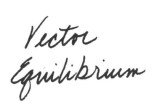

Vector Equilibrium

Remembering then our six units of vector edge,
I'm going to take one unit of quantum out of the icosahedron
which has the thirty edges of five units of quantum,
and just leave four. So what I have to do is go around
taking out one bar like that,
then I'm going to have to take out another bar over here,
and I come around and take out another bar over here.

And I go into the other hemisphere—I've taken out three so far—
so now I take one out here, and take this one out here.
That's five. I need one more to be removed, and here it is.

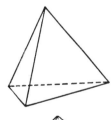

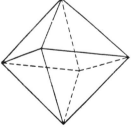

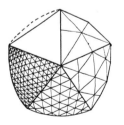

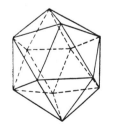

So we now have what we call the vector equilibrium with eight triangles and six squares. Now I'm going to articulate it. I'm going to take this top triangle and lower it to the triangle on the table; and the triangle on the table mustn't twist and the triangle up here musn't; just simply lower one towards the other.

As I start to do that, it suddenly becomes the icosahedron.
And I keep lowering, and the point stays out towards you,
and lower, lower, and suddenly it becomes the octahedron.
So we see a complete transformation from the icosahedron to the octahedron.
We see all the vectors have been doubled up, all the edges have been doubled up.
Now supposing this were a force; if I pull on it here, this forces it to contract.

Supposing this were revolving in space, a whole group of stars, another great star group here,
through mass attraction, simply retards this thing
and forces it to contract.
Suppose now, I see it coming around towards me like this,
in this direction. That would make this top suddenly twist, torque, and plunge through in this manner
to become a tetrahedron.

So now we've gone from the volume of twentyness to the oneness, throug a complete set of transformations: vector equilibrium through icosahedron through octahedron down to the tetrahedron, the three basic structural systems in the universe.

Now we'll unwind again,
up we come… back again to our friend, the vector equilibrium.
And we find that this pumps…
pumping, pumping, pumping, I call it the jitterbug,
but the center is not twisting. This point always stays towards you.
So the whole system is contracting symmetrically.
All twelve points approach a common center at a symmetrical rate.

Supposing, then, that you have pressure on the roof of a building.
You're used to the idea of the building flattening.
But when you put pressure on the top of the building here,
it means that the whole building contracts symmetrically.

The vector equilibrium contains the whole phenomenology of the universe

If we put one of these twelve vertices in the center, we have four hexagon

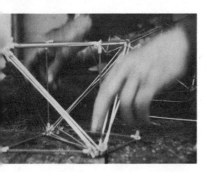

You can see a hexagon plane here at the center,
another hexagon plane here,
another hexagon plane here,
and a fourth one here.
Each one of those had six radii; the six radii,
or the twelve radii to these twelve points,
are equal in value to the cords,
because the hexagon's six edges and six radii are of equal value,
so that the tendency to explode and the tendency to contract are exactly balanced.
That's called "vector equilibrium."

It represents the closest packing of spheres around one sphere. A center sphere here, and twelve spheres around it, represent the basis of all atomic packings, and all the oscillations and wave phenomena that are articulated in our electromagnetic world.

The vector equilibrium is never witnessed by man;
it is as pure as God.
It is truth that is approached; it is exactitude that is approached.
The nearest thing
to the total patterning of all the patterns of complexity in the universe that we can find to the universe itself,
is man.

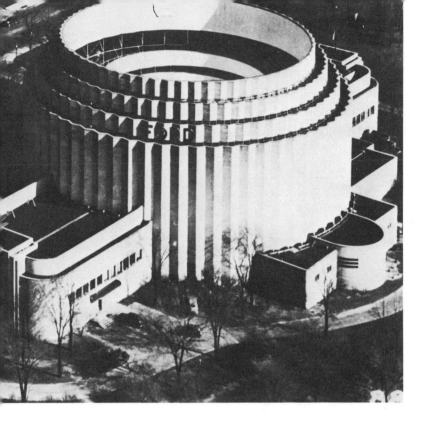

BUCKY FULLER FINDS A CLIENT

'oung Henry Ford translates the geodesic dome into aluminum and plastic, spans 93' rotunda

with 2½ lbs. per sq. ft. of floor area compared with 50 lbs. for steel

As announced in Architectural Forum *(May 1953)*

"The best architectural ideas and the best engineering ideas are stymied ór too often discredited as screwball or dream stuff until someone is willing to back them with his dollars and prove they are as practical in fact as they are exciting in concept.

"Take the case of Buckminster Fuller and his geodesic dome. For 20 years everyone has recognized Fuller as one of the most prolific idea men in architectural engineering. For 20 years everyone has said that some day somebody would revolutionize building by realizing Bucky's dreams.

"Ford was intrigued by Fuller's dome for three good reasons: The old Rotunda Building could not carry a 160-ton conventional dome of steel— 'the 60' tall cylindrical well would have split apart'—but it could easily carry the 8½-ton geodesic dome of aluminum…Fuller's photogenic structure is a public-relations man's dream.… The structure was assembled in 30 working days.… Fuller had to resort to what he called aircraft-building technology. The dome's many and interchangeable parts were factory cut and drilled to tolerances of 0.005". Elimination of on-site dimensioning and fabrication let Fuller carry aircraft tolerances over into the building field."

The basic unit, an aluminum alloy strut, three feet long and weighing only five ounces, 19,680 of which make up the 93-foot umbrella dome: struts make a triangle; three triangles make a tetrahedron; two tetras make an octa; twenty-five octas make a triangular octet-truss section; each pie-shaped section is laid into the growing umbrella.

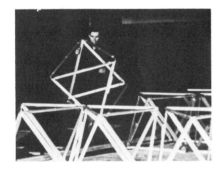

he dialogue between tetrahedron and evolving sphere is a union of
opposites. The impulse of energy that activates growth is riveted to its
opposite, control of growth; molecular tension seesaws with compression:
nature's breathing and regenerative process. Outward and inward space
respond to each other, sphere within sphere, swelling and opening to a
screening geometry of Gothic immateriality.

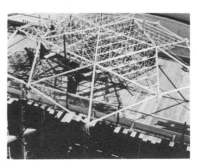

M.C. Sonnabend, my collaborator on the Titan, came up with a quotation from
Shakespeare that seemed especially appropriate for Bucky:

> The poet's eye, in a fine frenzy rolling,
> Doth glance from heaven to earth, from earth to heaven;
> And, as imagination bodies forth
> The forms of things unknown, the poet's pen
> Turns them to shapes, and gives to airy nothing
> A local habitation, and a name.
> —*Midsummer Night's Dream*, Act V, Sc. 1

As Sonnabend put it in our Sketchbook:

Eventually we dropped the first two lines. But bodying forth the forms of things
unknown, turning them into shapes, and giving to airy nothing a
local habitation—surely, that was Bucky; the name? geodesic domes.

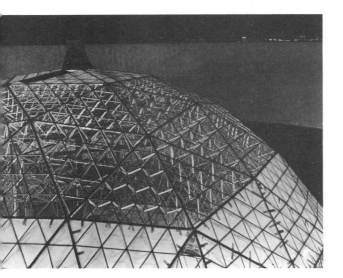

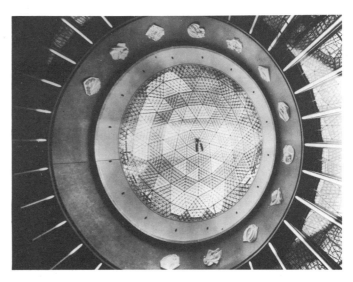

Bucky's "dream stuff" now finds "a local habitation and a name," the geodesic dome. As commissions start to come in from various government agencies and private sources, small and large, they begin to proliferate: any material—preferably the new, lightweight aluminum alloys or Fiberglas; any size or configuration—hemi-, three-quarter, five-eighth, full sphere; built inside out, as was the Ford dome; outside-in as the Wood's Hole dome; skin and bones become one in the Kaiser dome; skinless as the American Society of Metals structure.

Aspen Dome in Colorado and at Wood's Hole

The 36-foot, wood-strutted, plastic-skinned dome which we developed at the University of Minnesota; the students assembled it in an hour and a half at the Aspen, Colorado, Design Conference. It was then trailered to Wood's Hole, Mass., where, assembled with a canvas skin, it served as the shelter for the crew that worked on the dome restaurant Gunnar Peterson commissioned: a fifty-five footer, wood-strutted, mylar-skinned.

The dome rises with the controlled simplicity of a natural event—in-dwelling process takes outward visible form: a house, a spider's web, or a star.

*Dome Restaurant
at Wood's Hole*

In the Kaiser dome which was developed by my student, Don Richter, skin and bones are one—roof and wall blended—as the geometry is impressed into the aluminum pans.

Manufactured in Oakland, California, the 145-footer was erected in Honolulu in 22 hours. At the 22nd hour, the Hawaiian Symphony Orchestra and the audience of 1,500 persons were seated. Henry Kaiser flew in for the opening, but they beat him to it.

Kaiser Dome

The covering for the headquarters of the American Society of Metals, Cleveland, Ohio, is all framework, 250 feet in diameter. The hexapent, wire-wheel truss, double dome was erected by the North American Aviation Company.

A web of light carries the magnificence of Bucky's ideal to its most ethereal form. From out of the heart of his developing thought, the idea of cosmic growth, orbiting outwardly and inwardly, rises like a hymn in praise of order, pure sculptural form, a "roof of sky."

Keeping pace with such commercial commissions, to be sure, were the requests from various university architecture, engineering and design departments for Bucky to give design workshops. Here he tackled specific structural problems and experimental artifact solutions with the groups of students that flocked to participate. It should be evident that Bucky would not neglect the workshops for the commissions. Frequently, they ran pari passu; and, frequently, this led to crossed wires. Thereby, inevitably, hangs a tale.

The U.S. Marine Corps commissioned Bucky to do a "Lightweight Shelter Study" which involved prototype design and development of shelters and hangars for Marine Aviation advanced bases.

For this two-year undertaking, Bucky recruited as his principal assistant, James Fitzgibbon of the faculty of North Carolina State College in Raleigh, where Bucky had been a visiting professor. Simultaneously, he kept up his commitments to the growing number of college workshops around the country. He kept in touch with the work at Quantico, under the supervision of Colonel H. C. Lane and Fitzgibbon, by long, long-distance telephone calls.

On board the USS Leyte

One month, the Marine Corps found its communications budget going over the top, and a cautionary word went around the base. One of the Marine staff who faced a problem reached Bucky by phone at Tulane University and anxiously pleaded for a quick answer to a simple question; two hours later the crestfallen lieutenant hung up the phone.

"Dammit," fumed the administrative supervisor, "I warned you; now, if you have to talk to Bucky, we've got plenty of fuel, so fly to wherever he may be; but don't—and this is an order—don't telephone him!"

Despite the flaps, perhaps because of them, the project was successfully completed. In his official report, Col. Lane called the geodesic domes "the first major improvement in mobile military shelters in 2,600 years."

As Business Week commented: "On the ground, there was nothing particularly extraordinary about the shelter[!] which was 30 ft. in diameter, 15 ft. high, weighed 1,190 lbs., and could accommodate 30 men. The model was a five-sixth scale model of the planned type.

"What was extraordinary was that a standard Sikorsky HRS-3 helicopter hitched onto the shelter, hoisted it aloft in a 15-mph. wind, took it for a ride at 40 mph."

The N. Y. Times and Herald Tribune gave it front-page-left coverage: "Marines Try Out Flyable Shelter — 'Flying House' Is Carried By Marine Corps Helicopter." The Illustrated London News carried two photographs of the "portable hangar" under the page banner, "Notable Air News: Experiment, Achievement and Adventure."

'Dynamic' dome

A few of the experimental structures were even more Buck(y) Rogers than the Marines' helilifted domes: would you believe a "Dynamic Dome," a "Foldable Dome," the "Flying Seedpod," the paperboard "Disposable Dome?"

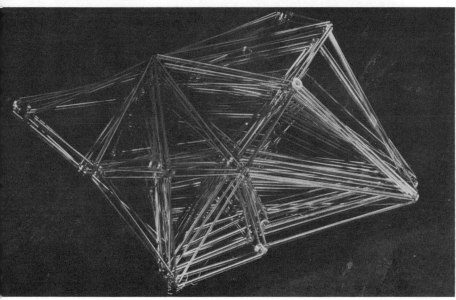

Foldable dome

A thirty-one-great-circle necklace of tubular beads on an internal thread of cable could be folded up in a tight package. When you unfold the necklace, it could be tightened at its equator until it's a rigid hemispheric grid-frame. We experimented with a number of these at Cornell, Oberlin, and the University of Michigan.

'Flying pod'

If somehow the beads of the necklace could be powered and the folded necklace flown and dropped—at Washington University, St. Louis, Missouri in 1954–55, the "Flying Seedpod":

Magnesium ball-jointed tripods (ball-jointed at their feet) were tensionally opened by piston-elevated masts, driven by 200-pound gas pressure in cylinders located at each vertex of the structure. As the wing-flyable bundl stood upright, a pulling lanyard permitted the 42-foot dome to open and erect itself in 45 seconds. I could foresee the development of air-droppab and rocketable remotely self-installable, controlled environments.

I was always fascinated by the lightest weight materials, such as paperboard; and we tried out a few—a small 30-footer at Yale University Architectural School; a larger one, coated with polyester resin, at Tulane, in '54; even one for the Marine Corps. Since the geometry—cut, folds, assembly instructions—could be printed on the corrugated Kraft paperboard sheets, it might one day be printed like a newspaper. Shoji and I rushed out a forty-two-footer for the U.S. entry in the 1954 Milan Triennale. It was installed in the garden of the Castello Sforzesco; furnished as a bachelor apartment, it won the *Gran Premio*.

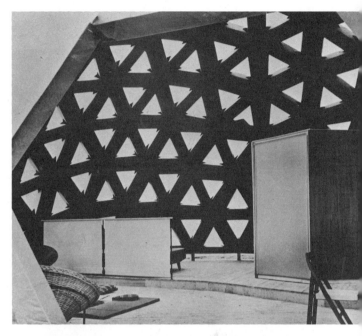

Paperboard dome:
Milan Triennale

To house the radar stations of its Distant Early Warning system, along the Arctic perimeter, the Air Force required a structure that could be flown and set up within a 24-hour weather margin, withstand a 150-mile-per-hour wind, and be radar-proof. Metal was out, so Bill Wainwright and I designed a polyester Fiberglas pan module.

The Radomes of the DEW-Line

With the success of the paperboard dome at the Milan Triennale, an international design arena, and the Fiberglas Radomes of the Air Force's DEW-line, the U.S. government's Office of International Trade Fairs recognized, as had Henry Ford II before it, the public relations as well as the practical values of the dome as an example of American ingenuity and more-with-lessing economy, against our prevailing image of wastrel less-with-more.

Tested on Mt. Washington

Trade Fair Dome

The 100-foot aluminum-tube frame is packed into one DC-4, flown to overseas site, and set up by unskilled labor within 48 hours after delivery. It was first installed for the Trade Fair at Kabul, Afghanistan. One American engineer directed the Afghans, who regarded it as a modern Mongolian yurt, and thus a native type of architecture. The grid-frame is dressed in white sailcloth. The dome was an instant hit and was flown back and forth as a show-piece to Tokyo, Poznan, the first trade fair behind the Iron Curtain, Kabul, Rangoon, and Osaka, Milan, Bangkok, Damascus, Lima, Casablanca…

The Trade Fair dome had so much built-in goodwill, that for its 1959 exhibit in Moscow, the U.S. government chose to impress with a 200-ft. Kaiser aluminum dome, gold anodyzed—and succeeded. The Russians were so impressed that they photographed every inch of external surface. The fact is that Bucky had earlier published the dome's mathematics in *Fortune* magazine which include a diagram of the clear-span dome dwarfing St. Peter's in Rome.

Anyway, it proved a pointless exercise, because in the end the Russians decided to purchase it. Premier Khrushchev is reported to have said, "Mr. J. Buckmingham Fuller must come to Russia and teach our engineers." (Peter Ustinov calls him Buckminster Cathedral—palaces and cathedrals; John Latouche, God rest his merry Dada soul, saw the pop man of the street, affectionately dubbing him, Fucky Buller).

Moscow Dome

Where weight is not critical, we may use steel, as in the Union Tank Car Roundhouse at Baton Rouge, Louisiana. Serving as a rebuilding plant, the Roundhouse was 384 feet in diameter and 116 feet high. The world's largest clear-span structure, it covered two and a half acres, more than enough for a football field and the running track around it.

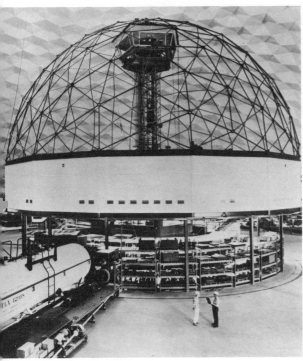

In the ensuing decades, Bucky's geodesic domes have covered more acreage on the earth's surface than any other single kind of shelter; as of now "some 300,000 of them," Bucky avers.

*A poem to domes: In 1958 I undertook to produce an experimental
half-hour magazine of the arts and humanities on film
with the editors of* Time, *for the art house circuit—this was before TV—
the actual "sight and sound of form givers of our time," Sketchbook No. 1.*

Quite fortuitously, the London Times Literary Supplement, *came
to the rescue with an historic special issue on American culture;
the colonies had arrived! Each of the lively arts was evaluated and
a handicap list appended; Balanchine and Graham;
Stravinsky and Copland; Faulkner, Salinger and Bellow; Pollack and
de Kooning, etc. Ecco: the contemporary American pantheon.
Artist de Kooning and composer Stravinsky were easy choices;
but what of architects? Frank Lloyd Wright was on top of that list, but
he was dead and we had decided against obits. That left Mies van der Rohe
and Bucky Fuller.
Mies seemed on the edge of past history, while Bucky was far out in the futur
Cranston Jones, who was then Architecture editor at* Time, *later wrote, "With
R. Buckminster Fuller…architecture for the first time has a designer who step
forth boldly into Einstein's universe."
But Bucky was my father-in-law.
My friends pointed out that I'd be damned if I did and damned if I didn't.
So I asked Bucky to do a little fireside chat on his philosophy
as a brief verbal platform from which a visual roll call
of his domes would emerge.*

o assure that Bucky's talk would be short, simple, and homely plain, I suggested
o him that he address his talk to his grandchildren, Alexandra and Jaime.
Ie loved the idea, a little a-b-c, then out to the Playsphere which we had just
ut together on our patio...and dissolve from the dome to a montage of domes.

ucky concluded what was meant to be a short, to-camera self definition, with:

must be able to convert the resources of the earth;
must do more and more with less and less
ntil I reach a point where I can do so much as to be able
o service all men in respect to all their needs.

reat!
Only we had run out of film, a ten-plus-minute magazine, on the critical turn,
So, in 1927..."
Ve asked Bucky to do a pick-up.
OK, but he couldn't read it, it would lose spontaneity. All right, he'd start with
short introductory sentence.
ood.
Ve went through three ten-minute film rolls before we managed to put together
satisfactory, even poetic, vignette.

hings get smaller and smaller.
o we get down to things you're not able to see separately,
ut we see them with big microscopes;
ve get down to cells and molecules,
nd then to much smaller things called atoms;
hen to the nucleus; then to electrons, protons, mesons, etc.

You remember the stars, that are very, very big?
That's the biggest pattern that you know about.
Then we get down to very, very tiny things,
even smaller than you can think about.
The big things we call "macrocosm,"
and the very tiny things we call "microcosm."
Atoms, or the all but invisible radiolarium;
starry heavens, or my dome at Baton Rouge,
or even your Playsphere outside—
all are part of the macro-micro patterning.
And you in your size are somewhere in between
the very big things and the very tiny things.

The Sixties:

Bucky is invited to Southern Illinois University, Carbondale, Illinois, as Distinguished University Professor. Quite appropriately, he and Anne build themselves a dome home, licensed by Pease Plywood, one of the first shelter applications of the geodesic dome. And he sets up personal headquarters for his growing world-around activities, also appropriately, over a travel agency in a small two-story office building.

Anne and Bucky build themselves a dome home

In the dome's benign atmosphere in the Midwest, he is moved to compose a song to the tune of ''Home on the Range''

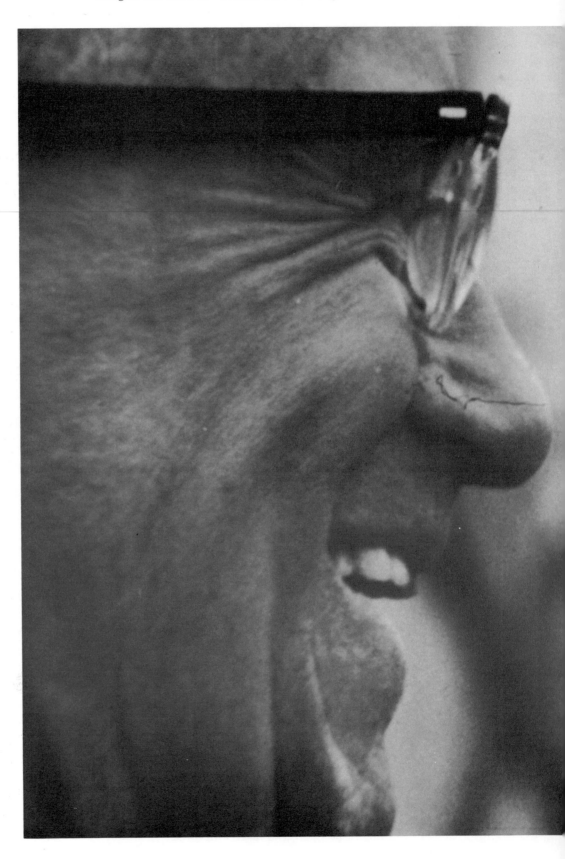

Roam Home to a Dome

There once was a square with a romantic flare,
Pure Beaux Arts, McKim, Meade and White;
In the mood that ensued, he went factory-nude
Mies, Gropy, Corbussy, and Wright.

Roam home to a dome
Where Georgian and Gothic once stood;
Now chemical bonds alone guard our blondes.
And even the plumbing looks good.

Let architects sing of aesthetics that bring
Rich clients in hordes to their knees,
Just give me a home in a great circle dome
Where the stresses and strains are at ease

Roam home to a dome
On the crest of a neighboring hill
Where the chores are all done, before they're begun
And eclectic nonsense is nil.

Let modern folks dream of glass boxes with steam
Out along super-burbia way;
Split-levels, split-loans, split-breadwinner homes
No down money, lifetime to pay.

Rome home to a dome,
No banker would back with a dime,
No mortgage to show, no payments to go,
Where you dwell, dream, and spend only time.

Indeed, the domes have a life of their own. Bucky spends more of his time doing research, writing, lecturing, consulting. His life is so public, the demands on his time so great, that to keep him straight on his schedule as well as to keep the growing numbers of family, friends, and colleagues in touch with him and occasionally cross paths on his to-ings and fro-ings, his office gets out a monthly itinerary. But this is not published to a mailing list: just as he does not talk-lecture except when asked to, so his itinerary is sent only to those who request it, a considerable network.

But as a rule, in order to reach this mercurial messenger as well as to get reprints of articles about him, for unpublished pieces by him, for copies of the map, etc., etc. one phones "mission control" or cables BUCKY, USA. This logistical support system has begun to swell to a large enterprise.

Because there are many readers who have, as I have, the common tendency to suffer jet-lag, or who may have respiratory problems, I forbear to excerpt from Bucky's itinerary. I will simply track a sampler of places or events in a two-week period. It could be any week, except, in the ensuing years, more so.

Around the world: Moscow, Montreal, Athens, Boston

This Timetable for a World Citizen encompasses the period of a few weeks during which: Bucky took off from Ontario after a meeting with the Prime Minister, a breakfast meeting, a lunch meeting, and a visit to Warner Lambert Canada Ltd. board room, a reception and dinner in Toronto, to arrive in Boston, Mass., at 11:56 a.m. He left Boston at 2:15 p.m. for Bangor to deliver the graduation address at Mt. Desert Island High School at 8 p.m. on June 9. Left for Ottawa on the tenth; flew to Dartmouth for commencement address, drove to Fairfield, Connecticut; flew from Fairfield to St. Louis, Missouri; from St. Louis to Carbondale, Ill., to San Francisco, to Los Angeles, to Tokyo, Japan—where he stayed put for a few days—arriving in New York in time to be guest of honor speaker at the annual United Nations Ambassadors' dinner. He left New York for Rome with a stopover in Paris, and flew from Rome to Cyprus to Athens, Greece, to speak at the Aegina Arts Center. Ferried from Aegina Island to Athens, he participated in Delos Symposium, left Athens, arrived in London and took off for Boston arriving on time to speak at the University of Massachusetts' Symposium on the Development of the Creative Human.

It's the likes of the Edisons, the Durants, the Millers, the Fullers that have convinced me that one of the secrets of genius, cause or effect, is to be able to catnap at will, standing, sitting, reclining. I've accompanied Bucky on planes and taxicabs and seen him pop out his hearing aids and, in a flash, be off and snoring. I've seen him arrive from far-off places, East and West, London, Tokyo, Australia, New Delhi, smilingly kiss all in attendance, excuse himself for a half-hour nap, and come bouncing back, fresh as a daisy.

N.B.: Bucky wears three wrist-watches for the major time zones; and he always carries at least five pens neatly clipped to his breastpocket: a black one for correcting proof or for writing, and four colored felt-tip ones for any sketches that he might make—and that would have to be color-coded for four-dimensional apperception—mostly on paper napkins or doilies in dining rooms on the ground, in the air, aboard ship. When he is chauffeured in a taxi or private auto, and one or another of his muses inspires him, an ordinary tissue will do.

An award he gave me on one occasion, I guess after I had done one of my films of him:

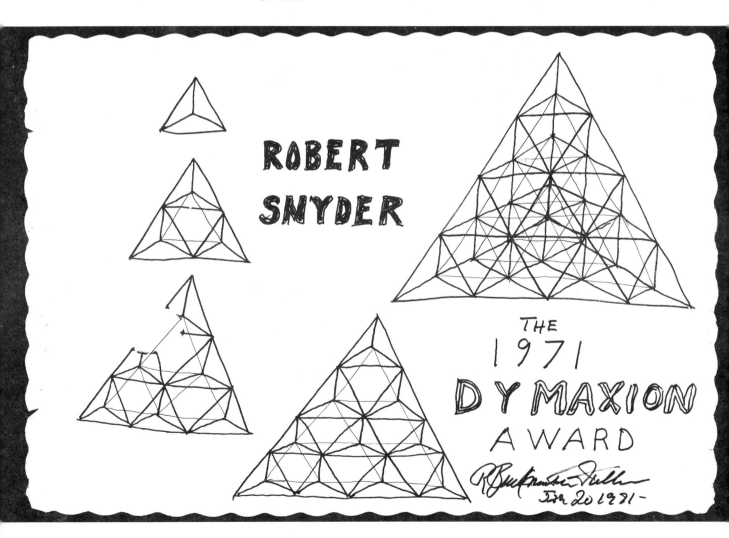

These are my headquarters.
What's going on here at my office is not only the accommodation of my own world-around activities, which are growing—I literally do live around the world—but at the university, I have this unique function of opening new frontiers, frontiers that are not within the accredited curriculum. It could be that the World Game which I'm developing here may become the whole curriculum of the university itself.

By playing the World Game and using the Dymaxion map as a distortion-free background, I developed the Inventory of World Resources, Human Trends, and Needs which is now housed in Philadelphia.
As the storehouse for all the information I've been carrying forwards over the last fifty years, it is quite prodigious
and has to be updated all the time.

1962: Some forty years after he had been "fired" from Harvard for the second time, Harvard appoints him Charles Eliot Norton Professor of Poetry, succeeding Stravinsky in the post. Shortly after, he is made an honorary Phi Beta Kappa by Harvard's Alpha chapter.

1963: Five of Bucky's books are published, on such subjects as economics, philosophy, mathematics, general business, science. The English have a word for such generalists, polymath.

1964: Time does a cover story, "R. Buckminster Fuller, The Dymaxion American." Bucky, very pleased, writes them, "I am deeply grateful for your generous treatment…if my life provided nought else but legends ultimately to inspire Artzybasheff's cover, my life is fully justified."

R. BUCKMINSTER FULLER

It felt more like me than any picture before made me feel. Interesting, because it had a geodesic-dome head, which my head is not; so it was not my head. Artzybasheff made the picture. I never saw him, but he sent three different photographers to Carbondale to make pictures of my eyes 'cause he said the only thing that counted was the eyes. I think he must have had over a thousand pictures of my eyes. Apparently he worked from there, because everything else is just formalized drawing. And as I say, it was me more than anything else, any picture of me I had seen before.

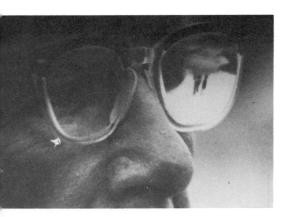

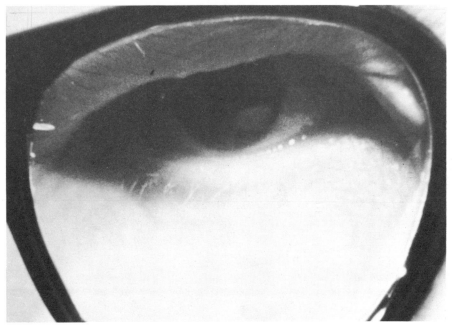

He was also very thoughtful about the things he included in the picture, besides my geodesic-dome head. He had the car, beautifully done, and he had all my favorite things. I don't know how he came to do that, but he really did know the things I cared most about.

I tried to buy the original painting but *Time* wouldn't sell it. They now have it in the National Portrait Gallery in Washington. *Time* donated a number of original covers to the Gallery which chose the ones it wanted.

World Game

From my earliest days in the water, and especially because of my experiences in the Navy during World War I
that led me to see our world as a spaceship, I was interested in maps and charts. More and more, with my continuing studies of world resources, I became increasingly concerned about an accurate map of the world.

We're all familiar with the Mercator map,
named for the Flemish geographer—of about 1594.
It's very useful in navigation, but that's where you find Greenland, for instance, three times the size of Australia—
which is the exact opposite of the truth—and the Mercator map has no Antarctic on it at all. I needed an accurate map. Why not just use a globe? Because you can only read a quarter of the surface at any one time. I wanted to be able to see all of it at once.

It took me two years, working with a wire frame of a spherical icosahedron wrapped around a world globe, to arrive at the point where I could unpeel the orange, spread it out, and the final map shows all the earth's surface without any visible distortion of the relative sizes or shapes of the continents. And because there's no break in the continental contours, as on other maps, my Dymaxion map shows a one-world island, in a one-world ocean.

Now, when you're studying population, resources, pollution and want to know percentages and put your information on a background that's very distorted like the Mercator map, you won't get a true picture. If, say, I find out where the demographic center for all human beings is and put pins on my Dymaxion map, each pin representing one-tenth of one percent of humanity where it actually exists, I get an accurate picture.

The same is true of resources;
an accurate background is fundamental to the study of world problems.
You can get a feel of it by just looking at how sparse the population is in
America, with the same kind of density in South America,
and then looking at the fantastic concentration of population
in England and Western Europe;
Italy—not so bad.
Then see the vast distances here, between Russia and India.
And then, when you get over here to this area, China—
boom! there's half of all humanity.

And in the same way we're pinning down economic data about increasing the rate of getting energy from here to there by electric network—or whatever the problem may be. With this kind of map study we're beginning to get enough insights about how you could make your whole world work for all humanity, very successfully.

Air-Ocean World

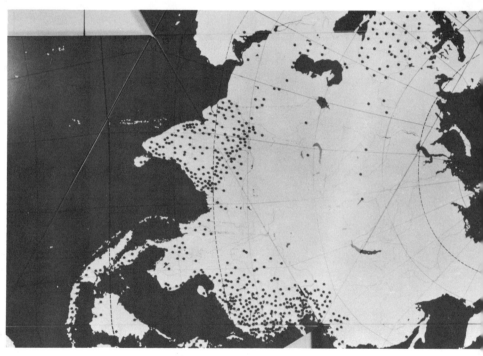

This water-ocean world is the way the world was to the great voyager-discoverers from Henry the Navigator down to the British Empire. At the turn of the century, when I was young, Kipling said, East is East and West is West, and never the twain shall meet.

And there they are: 53 percent of the world's population here, and the rest over there.

The people are way out at the perimeter; 90 percent of humanity is living north of the equator.

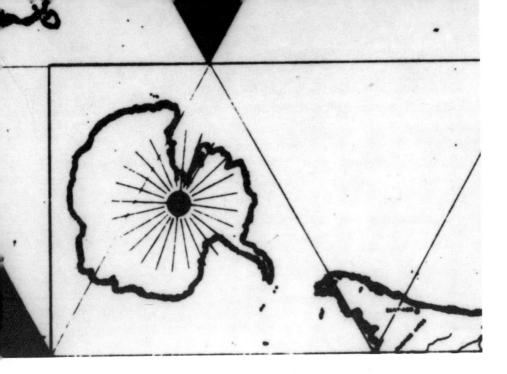

In this water-ocean world, notice the propeller blade in the center—nobody in here at all.

So the people who commanded this world
ran the merry-go-round of wind and water:
you come down from the Indian Ocean here
and get on the merry-go-round and come up in the Pacific;
get on the merry-go-round again, come up in the Atlantic;
get on again, come up in the Indian Ocean.
And what the British Empire commanded
was the southern tip of South America,
the southern tips of South Africa, Australia, New Zealand
—the great merry-go-round—and the people out on the perimeter
didn't know what was going on.

Ever doing more and more with less and less, the alloy chrome-nickel-steel
made possible the jet aircraft.
The jet, after all, was invented millions of years ago
by the squid or the jellyfish.
But when man tried to use the action-reaction for a jet take-off, the amount
of energy he had to release was so great and so hot that it shattered the engine
he had until he got to chrome-nickel-steel. This alloy has such high tensile

East-West world

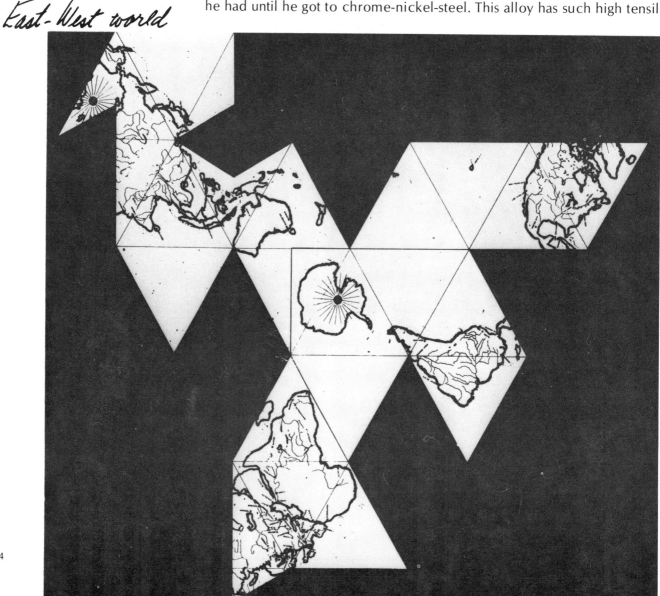

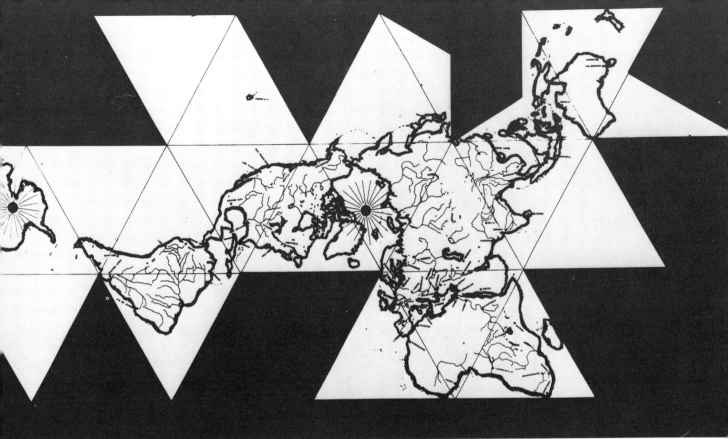

North-South world

strength at such high heat that it is really the essence that made the jet
possible in 1961—only yesterday.
It was then that three jets outperformed the Queen Mary in taking passengers across the Atlantic in one-third the time and for half the money. Ships of
the sea became obsolete as a way of man's getting from here to there. As a
consequence, we have an entirely new world.

Instead of having an east-west world, with men coming to harbors,
we suddenly have a north-south world, where, on the same map,
we find that 90 percent of humanity can reach each other
in the shortest great circle airplane route,
without ever going near the Atlantic, Pacific, or Indian Oceans.
Suddenly we have a completely new world.
In yesterday's world we had to have harbors—
therefore New York, San Francisco, and Seattle were very important.
And we had great railroads between them,
so everything was east-west.

I flew over New York harbor a few years ago and found in approximately a
thousand docks, only six ships—
and those freight yards in New Jersey, empty!
We have an enormous investment in humanity in the east-west harbor routes.
But in this new north-south world,
I go from India to New York in about the time
it used to take me to go from Boston to New York.

Delos

In the mid-sixties he is invited to attend the Delos Symposium, a summer gathering of distinguished thinkers such as Margaret Mead, Jonas Salk, Arnold Toynbee, Barbara Ward, et alia, hosted by Constantin Doxiadis, world-famous city planner and founder of ekistics, the science of human settlements.

The group meets at Delos, boards a chartered vessel which cruises the Aegean and holds its off-the-record seminars on the different isles of Greece.
And if there should be any local festivities, you may be sure that Bucky joins in, with gusto. On another trip the symposium celebrated Bucky's seventieth birthday.

Bucky's 70th birthday party

Bucky is elected to the World Academy of Arts and Sciences, the American Academy of Arts and Sciences, the National Academy of Design, in one fell swoop, and is awarded gold medals by the National Institute of Arts and Letters by the Royal Institute of British Architects.

Invited to attend the Spoleto Festival of Two Worlds, Bucky, with other of the stars in attendance—Henry Moore, Willem de Kooning, John Huston, Stephen Spender—made a Spoletosphere in which, as it was completed, a theater and dance happening was created.

Coincidentally, Ezra Pound emerged from his self-imposed silence to give a poetry reading. The two mavericks took to one another. Pound later inscribed a volume of his poetry to "Buckminster Fuller, friend of the universe, bringer of happiness, liberator." Although my contribution to this friendship was peripheral, I like to think I had something to do with its formation. A few summers earlier I had been invited to do a film portrait of Pound by Olga Rudge and visited Pound in Venice to show him Sketchbook No. 1: Three Americans. He was impressed with the Fuller sequence and so liked the logic of Bucky's domes that he said he would like to raise a small one on one of the tiny islands in the Venetian lagoon, and live in it.

This period is especially meaningful to me in terms of my filming him. We were commissioned by Chelsea House Publishers to make a half-hour film for their University at Large programs. Since "basic Bucky" now meant a direct exposition of his synergetics as well as a close-up view of his geometry, it was titled, Primer of the Universe, a more exacting portrait. We decided to film him during one of his relatively uninterrupted retreats at Bear Island.

1968

Filming Bucky

Noguchi, Pound, Olga Rudge, with Bucky at far right.

1969: He delivers the third Nehru Memorial Lecture in New Delhi; the subject, fittingly, is "Planetary Planning."
His staff assembles a first basic biography that fills twenty-seven pages.

Bucky's dome for the United States Pavilion at Expo '67 in Montreal is credited to Fuller and Sadao as architects. Shoji Sadao was one of Bucky's outstanding students at Cornell and stayed on with him, receiving credit on the Dymaxion map as well as the paperboard dome for the Milan Triennale.
Since Bucky did not consider himself an architect, and never applied for an architect's license, he could not take on any major architectural projects, such as the Expo Dome for the U.S. Pavilion, which required a "shing
Since such work was of major interest to Shoji—as the Radome had been to Bill Wainwright, the Kaiser dome to Don Richter, special projects to Jim Fitz gibbon—Bucky and Shoji set up an architectural firm.

The Expo Dome is a three-quarter sphere.
Inside the dome, the walls start going away from you;
this has an extraordinary psychological effect of releasing you, for
suddenly you realize that the walls are not really there.
Something is keeping the rain away, like an umbrella;
but you don't feel shut in, you feel protected.

I walked around and listened to what people in the crowd had to say,
and they seemed happy in this open but controlled environment.
And it was not done according to the aesthetics of architecture as it had been
practiced up until then. It was done simply in terms really of
doing the most with the least.

The Seventies:

Auspiciously inaugurating the 70s was the American Institute of Architects Gold Medal award to Bucky.

Bucky and Anne moved back East to Philadelphia; he has been made World Fellow in residence by a consortium of the University of Pennsylvania, including Haverford, Swarthmore, and Bryn Mawr colleges, and the University Science Center. His staff has swelled commensurately with the growth of his archives, the legendary Chronofile, his Inventory of World Resources, Human Trends and Needs, the embryonic World Game, and shelves of Dymaxion maps, books and reprints of magazine articles about him and by him.

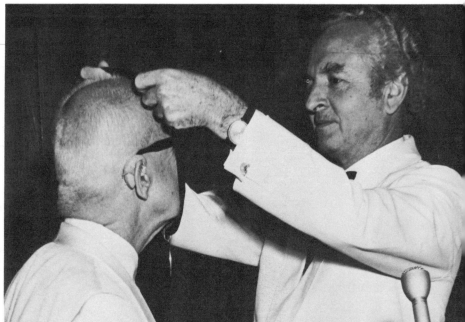

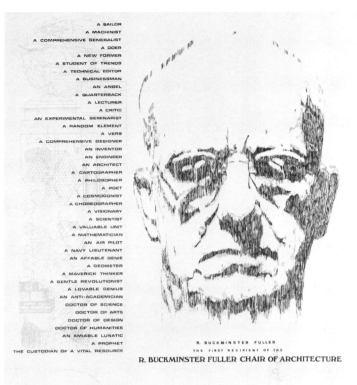

A SAILOR
A MACHINIST
A COMPREHENSIVE GENERALIST
A DOER
A NEW FORMER
A STUDENT OF TRENDS
A TECHNICAL EDITOR
A BUSINESSMAN
AN ANGEL
A QUARTERBACK
A LECTURER
A CRITIC
AN EXPERIMENTAL SEMINARIST
A RANDOM ELEMENT
A VERB
A COMPREHENSIVE DESIGNER
AN INVENTOR
AN ENGINEER
AN ARCHITECT
A CARTOGRAPHER
A PHILOSOPHER
A POET
A COSMOGONIST
A CHOREOGRAPHER
A VISIONARY
A SCIENTIST
A VALUABLE UNIT
A MATHEMATICIAN
AN AIR PILOT
A NAVY LIEUTENANT
AN AFFABLE GENIE
A GEOMETER
A MAVERICK THINKER
A GENTLE REVOLUTIONIST
A LOVABLE GENIUS
AN ANTI-ACADEMICIAN
DOCTOR OF SCIENCE
DOCTOR OF ARTS
DOCTOR OF DESIGN
DOCTOR OF HUMANITIES
AN AMIABLE LUNATIC
A PROPHET
THE CUSTODIAN OF A VITAL RESOURCE

R. BUCKMINSTER FULLER
THE FIRST RECIPIENT OF THE

R. BUCKMINSTER FULLER CHAIR OF ARCHITECTURE

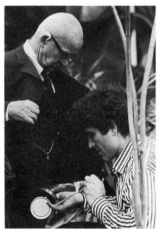

Bucky goes into orbit…and goes more conceptual. Rather than doing work-shops and slide-shows about his work, he does more "thinking aloud." At his lectures he is "averaging more than 1,500 people every three days."

The first R. Buckminster Fuller Chair of Architecture is established by the University of Detroit and Bucky is its first appointee. I film the events: racing after him to St. Louis, where he squeezes in a visit to his Climatron botanical gardens, back to headquarters at Southern Illinois University for a scheduled session with a group of President's Scholars, and out to Los Angeles for a talk there, because I have been commissioned to do a one-hour special for NBC's series "Experiment in Television." "Buckminster Fuller on Spaceship Earth" was well-received.

My subject is based on a very big picture of all humanity
going through a transition so unprecedented, so unexpected as to be really
very difficult to comprehend—
not just like going through the looking glass
where you get a reverse pattern of yesterday.
I can tell you that there are, at all times now, approximately 66 million
babies in the wombs of their mothers,
and 66 million is a very large number. Compared to the size of nations, it
would be the tenth largest nation in the world.
I think all of humanity is coming out of a sort of group womb of permitted
ignorance of man.

Permitted ignorance simply because it is in the nature of the total process
of regenerating life on earth that the new life be born

absolutely helpless and completely uninformed.
It has beautiful equipment, and is very ignorant.
When I was young, humanity was still 90 percent illiterate, and suddenly
we've gone to almost complete 90 percent literacy. Anywhere I go around
the world, people have good vocabularies,
and those good vocabularies got proliferated by radio that gets into the
homes— through schools—
and even more so by television, where by seeing the object
they can correlate the words and the image.
All of a sudden, we have communication capability.
We're gradually discovering we have an intellect,
an ability to acquire information,
and that there are very reliable behaviors of the physical universe
that can be employed.

Democracy certainly couldn't work as long as you have an illiterate group
that doesn't really know what's going on, leaving governing to a power
structure which has all the intelligence information and makes the decisions
without the people really knowing why.
So I say we're coming to this absolutely new moment when it could be that
phenomenon, democracy, really might work.
Now, with the information proliferation that's going on around the world,
this could become a possibility.
You are going to have to find out what needs to be done.
How do you organize yourselves to accommodate a growing humanity
that is now going to double or triple their lifespans,
to give them a chance to enjoy their earth?
That is the designer's responsibility.

Architects aren't doing anything!
They're perfectly willing to sit around drawing pictures and feel "If the pictures are pretty, that's enough!"
But you don't ever have to worry about beauty or pretty,
because if you really understand your problem, if you solve it correctly, and you do it so economically it is realizable,
it always comes out beautiful.
That's why a rose is beautiful.
It is just one of those parts of the great regenerative process of the universe.

If you want to be part of that, you can't miss beauty.
That part, your joy, will be there; your joy will be just as much as it is with a beautiful sunset.

One Xmas in the early seventies I had the rare pleasure of out-Santa-ing Bucky. I received a call some months earlier from a young man in Capistrano Beach, John Warren. He had seen our film The World of Buckminster Fuller, an expanded version of the TV special, and would like to show me, and he hoped Dr. Fuller himself, a little geodesic dome he had designed.

A couple of weeks later Warren, a former marine biologist, expert surfer and surfboard-maker, arrived at our home in Pacific Palisades with a friend in an old army jeep. Lashed to its back was a stack of sand-colored polyester-fiberglas pancakes. They unlashed the stack and cartwheeled each of the twenty-one 5-foot diameter hexapent pans up the side of the house to the back patio and laid them down flat in a circular pattern. I noticed that edges of the units were of two designs: slit 1½" troughs with three ½" holes spread equally along the center of the trough, the female, alternating with a single 1½" edge with three ½" pips protruding, the male. They began joining one pan's male to another's female and, tilting them upright, began to form an outer ring, and joined units onto the first ring, outside-in (like the Radome).

Within ten minutes, a lovely self-shingled, overlapping surfaced dome— "Turtle"—was standing firmly. We entered through the flip-top door and felt the lovely, quiet space.

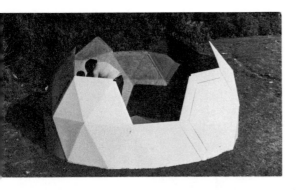

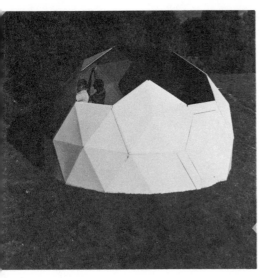

I thought, Bucky would arrive for the holidays after a Far Eastern swing, Tokyo and/or New Delhi, if not Sydney, Hong Kong and the Philippines, I forget. So I scripted a scene: As always, Bucky would come bouncing in with his beaming, toothy grin and chipper sailor-gait through our long living room, greeting and kissing us, the children, dogs and cats. He would pass the French doors outside which, on the grass ledge beyond the patio, sat the Turtle dome.

He would do a double-take, and would have to take a look. And so it came to pass: After the warm greetings, he came to a sudden stop, swung back, went out the doors, and his head rolling from side to side, muttering grunts of admiration as he "read" the structure, he came face to face with it: "I've been thinking about you for years." I pushed shy John forward, introducing him. Bucky embraced him and they went round and round the dome. Bucky punched and kicked its sides: "You can't break into this inverted boat hull; but if you had to, you could push out of it, unsnap it, easily enough!"

Bucky ordered a fistful of Turtles—a few for Bear Island, one for niece Kariska Kenison Pujarski's nursery school in Sausalito, another for Ruth Asawa's community garden project in San Francisco—and admitted John into his ever-growing and regenerating family of assistant comprehensive designers, putting him to work on improvements of the Turtle dome and such-like research and development.

His lectures and consultations continue to be given only to those who ask him to speak. And since he must be selective, his fees increase at a faster rate than inflation. On the other hand, and all too frequently, he will exact no fee at all from an inpecunious group, however small and humble. He squeezes in amongst government, corporate, university, trade association and national convention lectures, visits to an Immaculate Heart College, Watts Towers, a jail, a struggling progressive school, San Francisco's Alvarado School...

Southern California
Institute of
Architecture

I review planetary resources in terms of today's gained knowhow,
to see whether there's any way we might be able to do
much more with much less,
to be able to take care of everybody.
All political systems and wars based on scarcity would become obsolete.
World Gaming is played, not like checkers against an enemy
but against ignorance, inertia, and fear.

The World Game proves that John Von Neumann's theory of war gaming,
which holds that one side or the other must ultimately die,
either by war or starvation,
is invalid and offers
a heretofore unconsidered alternative way to play the war game
in which, as in mountain climbing, the object is
to find all the moves by which the whole field of climbers would win as
each helped the other
so that everyone reached the mountaintop successfully.

I think of my World Game as a way to bypass politics, human ignorance,
prejudice, and war and put the facts before man and the whole world to try
to deal with them coherently. We have never so far made the attempt
to take our collective destiny into our own hands, and shape it.

In the beginning of the nineteenth century, Thomas Malthus (1766–1834) was professor of political economics at the British East India Company's Haileybury College. At that time, this trading company was the most powerful organization operating in the three-quarters of our earth which i covered by water—and on a great deal of the land as well—having starte out in the sixteenth century as only one of many East India companies. Malthus was the first economist in the history of man to receive his vital statistics from all around our spherical planet, as the British Empire was on of the earliest spherical empires.

If we were living on a plane, as all the earlier empires from Alexander the Great to Genghis Khan conceived it, then it would go on to infinity and there'd be an infinite amount of resources with which to make up for anything we exhausted; and there'd be an infinite amount of room to get ri of anything we didn't want—such as pollution. The minute you discover you're not on an open, but on a closed, system, you find that suddenly there's no infinity, no resources.

Malthus

Malthus theorized, from the information he was receiving from all the courts of all the rulers of the world, that apparently man was multiplying himself at a geometric rate and producing goods to support himself at only an arithmetic rate. The implication of this theory was, quite clearly, that man was designed to be a failure and that only very few men could survive.

Darwin and other biologists and geologists were able to go around the world, taken by the great masters of the water-ocean, to discover what resources there were around our planet that a great mariner mightn't recognize, but that a great scientist could.

Darwin said, "This is a catalogue of all living species," and found some new relationships of vertebrates and so forth. He was then able to evolve a theory of evolution. Apparently the designing of these creatures was a consequence of the survival of only the fittest.

Incidentally, Darwin would not have been able to develop the theory of evolution at the time of the Roman Empire because it would have had to include dragons to the nth power!

So we have Darwin plus Malthus: nowhere nearly enough to go around an survival of the fittest. So the great masters of the water-ocean world, having mastery of the water, the best information, and the best beautiful fighting ships, said, "Obviously, we're the fittest."

Karl Marx agreed with their general theory of nowhere nearly enough to go around/survival only of the fittest, but he said quite clearly that the work is fittest because he knows how to handle tools; and all those other people are parasites. So this really brought about the concept of class warfare.

Karl Marx

Our world is still assuming that there is not enough to go around, and the basis of all our ideological battles—of both East and West—rests on this assumption, both saying: "We cannot guarantee that you're going to eat on our side, or that you're going to like it; but we have the fairest or the most logical or the most scientific way of coping with inadequacy." By virtue of which, in the last decade, the sum total of preparations for Armageddon by China, Russia, and the United States and NATO is billions of dollars a year—all trying for the highest capability of man to kill man.

Now I happened, by good fortune, to be in the United States Navy at the time of World War I and, in due course, became an officer of the line. In the Navy I began to be fascinated that we had airplanes, which we never had before, and we had electronics and alloys we never had before. The greatest secret of the Navy was doing more with less, where a little ship might be able to sink a big ship if it could move faster and outmaneuver it. In the late twenties, one little airship could sink a great cruiser. It was the beginning of a new era.

It could be, I thought to myself, that Malthus is really not pertinent today because he didn't know, for instance, that we were going to have refrigeration. I said, "What else did Malthus leave out?"
I began to inventory the many discoveries that were not available to him in 1810: there was no modern technology at all; no refrigeration; no production steel; no electromagnetics. He left out doing more with less. In 1917 I began to realize we actually had the possibility of doing so much with so little and might be able to take care of all humanity at the highest standard of living anyone has ever experienced, and to do it by 1985. And if we did that, the whole raison d'être of war would disappear.

The Navy played a "game," the war game. I decided to start playing what I called the World Game. Playing my World Game is a design revolution in contradistinction to a bloody revolution and the idea of getting on by just killing each other and seeing who survives.

Public lectures around the world

The World Game employs design science to produce progressively higher performance per units of invested time, energy, and know-how for each component function of the world's resources. It makes it possible for intelligent amateurs to discover, within a few weeks of studying simulated design revolution illustrated on the world map, that its premises are valid and to find specific ways in which they can be applied.

Now you don't play the World Game by saying, this is the scenario, and making some moves on a table. What you have to do is to develop competence in terms of technology; you have to understand how to design something more with less. Take, for instance, something like communication:

A man at the time of Malthus who wanted to send a message locally had to send a messenger on a horse; or, to send it around the world, a great big shi had to get him there. It took a great deal of energy and weight to get a message from here to there, and it was very slow.

Now, by radio and electronics, we obviously get a message around the world very much faster with very little energy or weight. With the first telephones you had one message going along a given cross-section of wire Then a few years later, we learned to get two messages over the same cross-section of wire simultaneously. Later on we got twelve messages on the same cross-section; then, twenty-eight; and two hundred and thirty to two thousand. It then went wireless, no wire at all.

And today we have one communication satellite, weighing a quarter of a
ton, outperforming the transoceanic communication capability of a hundred
and seventy-five thousand tons of copper cable! This is typical of the way
you do more with less.

This is the new world that's come in.
And when I talk about the ability to do more with less,
I see we're terribly tied up with all kinds of old ways.
Think of the fantastic amount of real estate involved here
that's absolutely obsolete!
The whole idea of property begins to go,
because you used to have to guard the trees and the vegetation
and you don't have to anymore.
You used to have to guard the mines.
You don't have to anymore.
Metals are now recirculating in great numbers,
except for a few of the new, rare metals.
Of steel and copper and aluminum, the main metals,
we have ample already in circulation.
This is exactly what Japan learned during World War II.
By getting all our scrap just before the war began,
they could get along without mines.
All we have to do is continually recirculate the metal,
and every time we load it with more know-how,
taking care of many more people and very much greater tasks.
So this whole World Game is really a design revolution.

We have internal and external metabolics. The energy necessary to keep human life going we call internal metabolics. Until recently, with horses and man doing all the work, primary energy was consumed internally, by man. This last year, however, only 1 percent of all energy produced on earth was and is being, consumed internally by man; and 99 percent is going into task outside which flows through mechanical systems.

After studying all of man's internal and external metabolics, you come to realize that what we call wealth is the capability of keeping life going.

It cannot be spent backwards; it cannot reorder one iota of yesterday. In this century we have learned that the physical part of wealth in the univers tends to regenerate; and the metaphysical can only increase: Every time you make an experiment, you learn more, not less. The physical part of wealth in universe cannot decrease and the metaphysical can only increas

So, every time we use our wealth, it increases—which is the exact opposit of our economic thinking that is based on depreciation.

To understand about design revolution, we have to ask, "How efficient are our uses of energy?" The reciprocating engine, for instance, is only 15 percent efficient; the turbine engine is 30 percent, or twice as efficient; now, the jet engine is 60 percent efficient; and when we get to the fuel cell it's 85 percent efficient.

The way we are using our engines is most inefficient. At all times in the United States around two million cars are standing in front of red lights, wit their engines running. Millions of horses in motion—going nowhere!

Out of every hundred barrels of petroleum we are taking into our econom 95 percent goes down the flush. We get only 5 percent. Clearly then, we don't have any energy crisis whatsoever. We simply have a crisis of ignorance; irresponsible, highly reflex-conditioned ignorance.

*Another former student-apprentice, Michael Ben-Eli, developed a project in New York
City where youngsters from East Harlem and the Lower East Side experimented with
paperboard and ferrocement geodesic structures for low-cost shelters.*

In great cities like New York or Chicago and Los Angeles
we have a fantastic amount of destitute humanity,
with people greatly demoralized,
trapped in the pattern of yesterday's ignorance.
There is nothing more exciting to me now
than that on those streets in the communities
I find leaders emerging
who, with a very deep and intuitive awareness,
want to make things work.

To my amazement, I found myself being asked for help
by gang leaders in Chicago, New York, and Los Angeles.
At first, when I came to meet them
my language scared them; they shied away.
But they came back to develop projects with
some of my young associates and students.

This group in New York, in particular,
was once a part of the Real Great Society.
Now it's called CHARAS,
and can stand up with great calm and say,
"We have got heads on our shoulders
and we can use them to work out something new
and useful."

The CHARAS group caught on intuitively
that they are endowed from birth with great intellectual capabilities
that they can really employ,
even though they never did go through school.
They are a prototypical operation of human beings,
able suddenly to master control of the environment
and to realize that they are themselves going to make breakthroughs.

My young Israeli friend, Michael Ben-Eli,
who worked with me and with students in Africa
and in other places around the world,
was able to teach and work with them so that
within four months they actually acquired
spherical trigonometry and were building their own
geodesic dome.

The honorary degrees and awards keep rolling in. His "basic biography" has, as of 1978, doubled in size; and a new section has been added: "New York Times Listings About or Mentioning Buckminster Fuller".

With the assistance of E. J. Applewhite ("Sonny") he begins to prepare for publication of his life's work, his energetic-synergetic geometry. The odyssey of this effort of a few years—its writing and editing, visions and revisions ad infinitum on planes, airports, hotel rooms—is wonderfully recounted in Sonny's book, Cosmic Fishing. Macmillan finally published the hefty tome Synergetics: Explorations in the Geometry of Thinking by R. Buckminster Fuller in collaboration with E. J. Applewhite.

Samuel Eliot Morison's review letter to Macmillan is worth quoting:

"Bucky Fuller's newest book, Synergetics, is his most important and most readable. He fits very well the description Thomas Carlyle wrote of another, about a century ago: 'This man is of the sort we now call original men, men of genius and such like, the first peculiarity of which is they communicate with the universe at first hand.' In this book, Fuller is writing for the general public and he gets 'down to Earth' by constantly indulging in homely comparison. Take his paragraph 400,10, for instance:

'The difference between infinity and finity is governed by the taking out of angular sinuses, like pieces of pie cut out of surface areas around a point in an otherwise absolute and infinitely extendable plane, and joining together the open gap's radial edges. This is the way lampshades and shirts are made'.

"From infinity, we are down to pie, skirts and lampshades!"

Fly's-Eye Dome

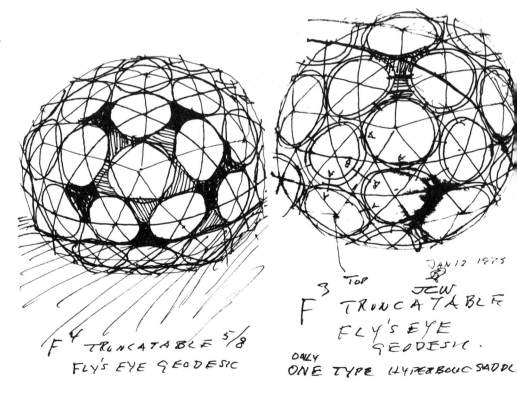

F⁴ TRUNCATABLE 5/8 FLY'S EYE GEODESIC

F³ TOP JCW TRUNCATABLE FLY'S EYE GEODESIC. ONLY ONE TYPE HYPERBOLIC SADDLE
JAN 12 1975

The "homely similitude" of Bucky's minister ancestors. Morison advisedly stresses "down to earth." Bucky's thinking-alouds...

Bucky says "it's my last artifact"—he should say artifacts, for on the heels of the success of Synergetics, he and Sonny undertook volume two — perhaps only the last conceputal artifact at that; for shortly he creates another revolutionary structural one, the Fly's Eye dome (doubtless he has a number of others up his sleeve, but he doesn't like to talk about them until he's prototyped and demonstrated them: they'll speak for themselves).

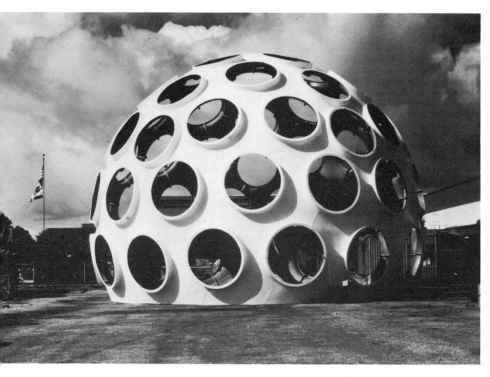

Because the dome is all lenses, it looks like a fly's eye. The joining of the fiberglas structural members creates the lens openings, much as the ring of dough creates the hole in the doughnut or the bagel.

I would never try to reform man—that's much too difficult. What I would do was to try to modify the environment in such a way as to get man moving in preferred directions. It's like the principle of a ship's rudder, which is something I thought a lot about as a boy here on Bear Island.

The interesting thing about a rudder is that the ship has already gone by, all but the stern; and you throw the rudder over, and what you're really doing is making a little longer distance for the water to go round. In other words, you're putting a low pressure on the other side, and the low pressure pulls the whole stern over and she takes a new direction.
The same in an airplane—you have this great big rudder up there, with a little tiny trim tab on the trailing edge; and by moving that little trim tab to one side or the other, you throw a low pressure that moves
the whole airplane.

And so I said to myself, "I'm just an individual, I don't have any capital to start things with, but I can learn how to throw those low pressures to one side or the other, and this should make things go in preferred directions, and, while I can't reform man, I just may be able to improve his environment a little.
But in order to build up those low pressures I'm going to have to really know the truth."
The child is really the trim tab of the future.

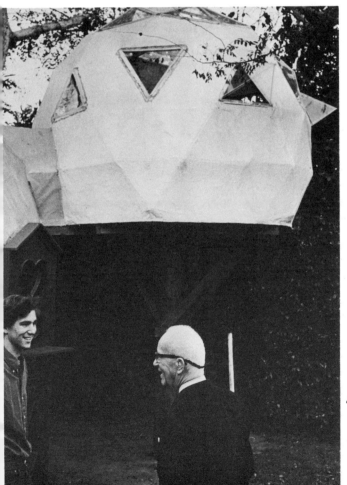

Bucky giving
. . . and receiving

Brooks Zeitlin's Treehouse Dome

Children are spontaneously truthful.

They used to be told, "Never mind what *you* think."
Now they're doing their own thinking,
so I feel that the young world is absolutely overwhelmed by the fact
that the world is a mystery.
They have a deep reverence for whatever truth and love may be.
We'll make it on our planet because of youth and truth and love.
Human beings are born naked, helpless, ignorant, and curious.
We now know we have been aboard our planet for about 2½ million years,
and we've had to go through a great deal
from being naked to the elements
to learning by trial and error, without words.
Now we have beautiful verbal communicating capabilities
and a great deal of knowledge.

We are able to explore the universe
telescopically, photographically,
to 1½ light years around our planet.
We photograph atoms.
Now we've reached the point of discovering that muscle is nothing,
mind is everything.
Evolution is integrating us
and we're no longer so remote from each other.
Clearly we are here to use our minds,
to be information gatherers in the local universe,
problem solvers in relation to the maintenance
of the integrity of the eternally regenerative universe.
Muscle is nothing; mind is everything.
But muscle is still in control of human affairs.
In about ten years, if we come out with muscle in control,
we will have chosen oblivion;
if we come out with mind in control,
it's going to be utopia and eternity.
Yes, we do have the option to make it,
but it's absolutely touch and go,
a matter of the integrity of every human being from now on.

Either you're going to go along with your mind and the truth,
or you're going to yield to fear and custom and conditioned reflexes.
With our minds alone
we can discover those principles we need to employ
to convert all humanity to success
in a new, harmonious relationship with the universe.

I'm not trying to imitate nature, I'm trying to find the principles she uses.

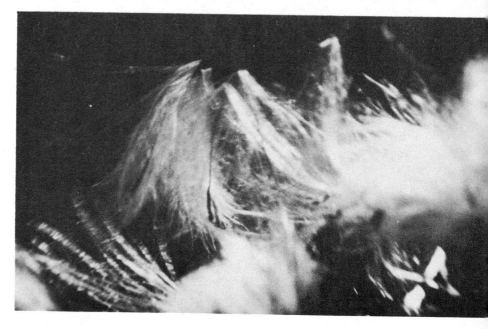

WHY NOT?...

People often tell me I'm an optimist, and I say, "I'm a very hard realist." I know we have the option to make it, and that's very different from being an optimist."

Print Houses on Paper

Why not print a house on paper?
There's no way a man can produce material for enclosures more rapidly
than on the great paper-making machines.
Add the printing press,
and you can put some important mathematical information on the paper.
So it's perfectly possible
—and we've tried it out—
to make what we call "paperboard domes,"
where you print beautiful mathematics right onto the material,
folding lines, and so forth.
Fold and staple; fold, staple...
and up she goes.
We can now produce, on just one paper-making machine,
the materials for 3,000 houses a day;
and they would cost about 5¢ a square foot
as against $2 a square foot for our usual kind of enclosure.
Made of the best Kraft paper,
with very high wet tensile strength and very high wet compressive strength,
these enclosures can last as long as any homes we've been familiar with.

Fold...

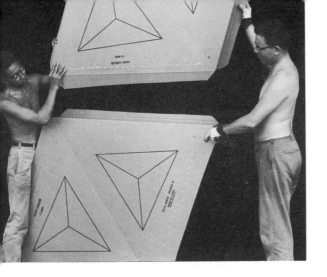

... staple

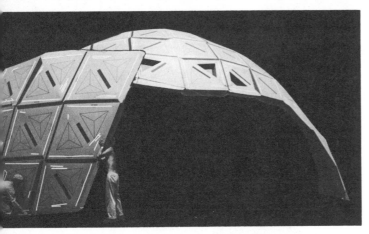

...and up she goes!

If, then, you also had an energy package,
a ''black box'' that took care of all your human functions,
all the processes which, on earth, are taken care of by the ecological
balance of nature
—which is just what the astronauts have in order to live in space—
man would be a success anywhere in the universe.
We figure about 500 pounds is the limit of the black box,
not much bigger than a good-sized suitcase.

This box, which originally cost some twenty-billion dollars,
will be made out of very familiar metals, lightweight, of course;
on an aircraft basis, it's worth about $2 a pound, or
a thousand dollars total. This $1,000 box,
because it will not deteriorate very rapidly,
could be amortized in five years;
so we'll say it costs $200 a year to buy it.
You get your $200 black box and you go off, with a geodesic paper-board
dome, anywhere you want,
where there's no high pressure of living.

Now who's going to pay the high rents one has to pay today?
In effect, man with his space umbrella and his briefcase blackbox
can go anywhere he wants to in the universe
and enjoy the very highest standard of living.

I find humanity being incredibly careless and thoughtless in using water. Human beings go to the toilet and get rid of one pint of liquid by using four gallons of water to flush the toilet.

Nature's got the sun to atomize the water into the sky so that it can come down on the mountain tops and into the lakes, and come our way. We are using it very carelessly. Nature is very careful. Nature clearly separates the liquids and solids in mammals, and we keep mixing them up again in the toilet bowl.

No scientist has ever been commissioned to discover the best way to dispose of beautiful human waste.

Cities are obsolete; absolutely.
Humanity is always going to be coming together, but not in static cities. The
cities where you grew up were based on trade routes we're no longer
using.

I don't want to talk about urban sprawl; I know human beings did what
they did with great earnestness. They were really doing their best within
their limits. And I realize they can't improvise and go against their city
building codes.
But real estate manipulators exploit conditions, saying, "People have to
come in here and the land is scarce so I'm making money."
Today you have enormous exploitation.

When I was young, 90 percent of Americans were on farms; now it's only
7½ percent. The people moved to the city for some kind of manufacture
that's no longer there.

The minute we get into disarmament—which we will—then all the highest
capability of man now going for armaments will be at the disposal of
livingry. Then, suddenly, we'll be creating a whole city in one day, and
removing it the next—just as you bring a fleet of ships into harbor one day
and out the next.
The concentrated meeting of humanity will not be given up at all, but we'll
get out from under the moneymaking and the exploitation of humanity in
the cities.

A number of people are now talking about roofs over cities; and it's getting
to be accepted in bigger plannings; so it's getting into the lingo....

The St. Louis Botanical Gardens Climatron is a Garden of Eden; it's very small compared to a roof over a city. But it certainly opens up thoughts about such larger undertakings.

Every time you double the size of a dome you get twice as much surface, but eight times as much volume. This means that the volume of molecules gains twice as fast as the surface. So if you double the size of the dome the amount of surface a given molecule inside could gain or lose heat is exactly half, and your energy conservation goes up very rapidly. When we cover something the size of a city, the energy conservation will be such that the great problems we're having about heat control, air conditioning, snow removal and the enormous energy needs involved will be greatly reduced. In a dome of city size, you wouldn't be aware of the grid at all; it just wouldn't be quite as bright as normal.

A Whole Navy Station under a Dome

A geodesic dome becomes the centerpiece of the new Amundsen-Scott South Pole Station.

Fabricated by Don Richter's Temcor, the 54-foot-high, 164-foot-diameter structure serves as a wind and snow screen for a complex of three prefabricated aluminum buildings that huddle beneath it. The dome provides an open-span, pleasant work atmosphere and, even more important, protects the station's people and equipment from Spaceship Earth's harshest elements.

Operation Deep Freeze was losing both people and equipment to the elements; so, cap the whole establishment with a dome.

Naval Facilities Engineering Command's design parameters were intimidating. The ideal South Pole shelter should:
- be exceptionally lightweight for easy transport by ship and plane;
- break down into components that could easily be sized for air shipment by LC-130s in a limited number of flights on the last leg of the polar journey;
- consist of materials that maintain their strength at extremely low temperatures;
- be large enough to accommodate the three 2-story structures to be erected inside it, with room to spare both for habitability and for future expansion;
- be comparatively easy to erect under adverse weather conditions; and
- prevent heat loss from deforming the interior structures.

The geodesic dome more than met them.

Why not ...

Sky-floating geodesic spheres?

Floating tetrahedronal cities?

Floating cities?

What we should be doing is guarding our antiquities from the elements and from vandals by placing a dome over them. Until now, people took their great antiquities apart and carted them off to museums. I've been asked to put domes over the oldest diggings in northeast Thailand where they found the earliest beginnings of the Bronze Age.

UNESCO had been asked to do something about the Parthenon which is actually disintegrating. UNESCO recommended taking it apart completely and putting all the parts into museums, replacing the real building with a fake. This infuriated the Athenians and they decided to ask me to put a dome over the Parthenon and have the museum in place.

The dome would have to be transparent so everyone would be able to see the Parthenon very nicely while it would be able to guard it from the inclemencies of the weather, pollution, bird droppings, and even from vandals.

What I would like to see happen, and what I think is going to happen, is a rebuilding of the Athenses and the Babylonias of history by reclaiming all the antiquities from the museums of the world and bringing them back to where they should be. Then we'll be able to go to them, traveling not only geographically but also in time, as we now go to Pompeii. Archeologists and anthropologists would be able to live there, reconstructing the life of yesterday.

People used to say, "You can't take it with you." Ownership used to be very desirable; now ownership is becoming onerous. Instead of spending enormous amounts of money keeping private museums the owners are not even living in any more, they're all going to want to give the things back to museums and the museums will give them back around the world.

The new world that's coming in
is an invisible world of doing more with less.
We're soon going to have beamed power, and no wires at all.
And then, when you begin to have the autonomous dwelling itself,
you'll stop having fixed buildings
and carrying enormous amounts of power to it.
You'll generate your own power locally, as at the airport,
instead of as you do. When a great airplane comes in, it's like a small city.
Up comes a small truck with the generators
and turns the whole thing on—charges it.
Up comes another truck with its air conditioners.
We don't need to build wires and pipes into concrete buildings;
we can move the power around to where it's needed.

Thinking about humanity on board our planet, the Spaceship Earth, and
playing the World Game, I became fascinated by the question, "How do we
get energy from here to there to help each other?"

If you look at the world map, you could see, not only crossing time zones
and reaching Alaska, where the Russians are putting up dams, hydroelectric
dams, in all their northerly flowing waters—all the way over there!
I suddenly found I could reach the Russian network—1,500 miles. Boy! this
would mean something because of all that standby power—that is, at
off-peak times when 50 percent of the generating capacity is not being used.
I found then that by integrating these networks to produce a global energy
grid, we could integrate night and day and *double* the generating capacity
operative around the world—immediately.

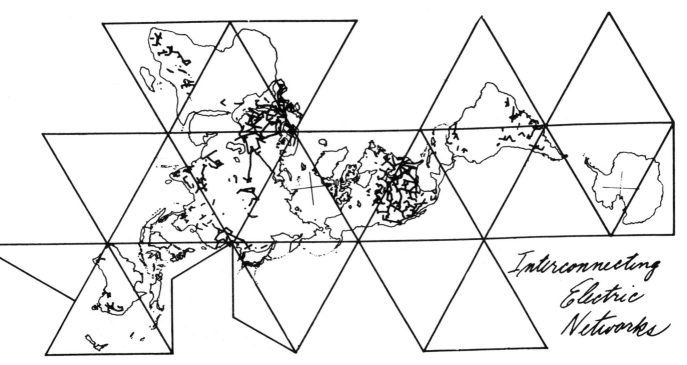

Interconnecting Electric Networks

**INTERCONNECTING ELECTRIC NETWORKS/1968
220 KILOWATTS**

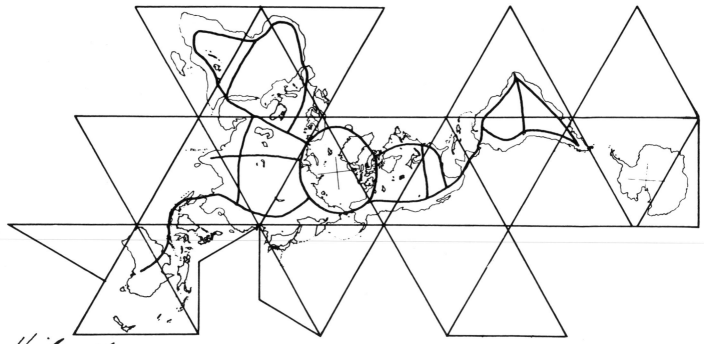

High voltage transmission network (projected)

Until recently, there was no way to get energy from here to there in large amounts except by wire, by electrical conductivity. The further you want to deliver it, the higher and higher do you have to raise the voltage. The higher the voltage, the more insulating problems will you get, and so forth. We only got into really large electrical energy distribution at the time of World War I when we discovered much better insulating devices and got into cryogenics with really no energy losses at all.
We got ultra-high voltage, and it became practical to deliver energy electrically over 1,500 miles, instead of 350.

The best customers that power companies have are industries. And they discovered that to hold their industrial customers, public utilities had to anticipate increased uses, for if the industrial customers turned on the juice and didn't get it from the public utility, they'd go and put in their own energy production plants. So the utility company had to study the needs of their customers, and they have the most incredibly accurate charts of when the peak loads come in every day of the year, every minute of the day.

The utilities have standby power for peak hours. This excess power is always being generated at a loss—a complete loss. But the company discovered that if it hooked up its wires with the next town's, where the peak loads occur at just a little different time of day or night, what had been a complete loss could go over there and become a profit. With interlinked networks, the loss could be turned to a profit. But within 350 miles, the company couldn't cross time zones. When it reached 1,500 miles it suddenly was able to go right across the time zone to a different peak time; which meant, of course, that there was a much better chance of selling that standby power.

When I was doing the World Game in 1969 with students for the first time in New York, I gave them this world network problem. They found it very exciting and developed it so that you could really see what is meant by a design-science revolution—comprehensive anticipatory design science; they really applied it that way. They found you could have a world network and it would double the generating capacity overnight. The heck with the money side—what we really want is to harness that energy and make it work.

I took this to Prime Minister Trudeau of Canada who is a good friend. About five years ago he was asked to go to Russia for the first time to meet Brezhnev. I gave my world map with the electrical energy network to Trudeau and he took it to Brezhnev and Brezhnev gave it to his experts. Trudeau came back and said the Russians absolutely loved it—it was great. They could see it extend immediately into China and around the rest of the world, integrating the night and day of humanity.

It was my first World Game, and we kept having sessions at different places. We had two at the University of Southern California and we carried on for three years at Southern Illinois University, three years at the University of Pennsylvania and we're doing it again every year.

At the World Game in Pennsylvania we did a complete
study of the energy of our earth, all the different types of resources and so
forth, and were able to publish a book. This book was done exactly the wa
they did the Apollo project: "What are all the things that have to be done
get human beings to the moon and back, safely?" So there's a book on
energy now, called *Energy, Earth, and Everybody,* written by Medard Gabel,
who led the project. I wrote a little introduction and Stewart Brand wrote
epilogue. In sum, the book shows how using only proven resources, prove
technologies, and proven rates at which technologies can be produced ar
put into place, all of humanity can enjoy as high an energy income as that
enjoyed exclusively by North Americans in around 1972 within ten years
starting to do it, while phasing out all the fossil fuels and atomic energy.

Looking at our total resources, we realize that the physical universe is all
energy—energy associated, which is matter, and energy dissociated, whic
is radiation—and that one is convertible into the other.
Universe is 100 percent efficient; syntropic here, and entropic there, but r
energy created, no energy lost.

During the time of the New Deal attempts were made at providing electri
power to rural areas like the Tennessee Valley which the private sector w
not interested in backing. The government built dams and turned all the
energy of what used to be disaster floods into low-cost energy for the
poverty stricken area.

The government put in enormous networks for that rural electricification.
When it came to the business of integrating across time zones, it was
discovered that the government networks would have to be integrated wit
existing private networks. It was lucky that we had computers, because the
problem was put to the computer: Which way would the private sector
make more money—by integrating with the government network or not?
The answer came back clearly: they'd make 30 percent more profit
integrating. And from a fixed kind of position, they yielded very rapidly.

Because the power of tides is gravitational power,
it could also be the highest order of energy—
and it would be pollution-free.
Electrical energy—its production and distribution—
is one of the world's critical problems;
but by constructing a worldwide energy grid,
spanning continents and hopping over oceans,
the whole thing can be tied to the power of the tides.
It's feasible now:
an international network that would integrate night and da
spherically cycling, shadow-and-light zones of Planet Earth

We could put to 24-hour use
the now only 50-percent-of-the-time-used
world-around, standby, generator capacity
whose 50 percent unused capacities
are now required only for peak-load servicing
of local, interconnected energy users.

Such intercontinental network integration would overnight
double the already installed and in use electric-power generating capacity
of our planet.

Because the wind is sun generated and is easily available locally, it is poten-
tially capable of supplying large amounts of pollution-free energy. In about
1970, growing out of the World Game group, Hans Meyer supervised our
wind study in Wisconsin, called Windworks.

They developed a windmill with propellers going round that generated
direct current—which is more efficient by 50 percent than in and out of
storage batteries. But all our electrical networks are on alternating current,
so they developed a much better circuitry for converting direct current into
alternating current. They also developed much more sensitive meters than
had been used up to then and persuaded the public utilities of Wisconsin
to allow them to go right into the alternating current and feed it into the
power lines.

The utilities company paid them for putting it in at only wholesale rates, and charged the public at retail rates to take it out. The company made money alright, but so did Windworks. The point was that you didn't have to have that 50 percent loss of going in and out of batteries.

A Wisconsin congressman was impressed and he began talking about it in Congress. Within a year and a half, twenty-two utilities companies in twenty-two states were allowing them to hook up their windmills.

Since the wind is always blowing within a 100-mile radius, we might get a total pattern of all the windmills we could be producing around the world, making it possible for the individual to begin to break the great power bind without getting any opposition from the money side. Money, and the business of making political hay and profits for huge corporations, is shortsighted. Being interested only in putting a meter between human beings and the wind won't get all the things done that need to be done.

The eons of cosmic energy wealth deposited in earth
as a future savings account in this little planet
is being depleted in one spend-thrift century.
The world's free enterprise cartels are determined to establish
comprehensive atomic energy power before the world's petroleum is
exhausted based on their conviction that humanity cannot
possibly conceive of any possible alternative to their atomic energy plans.
But options do exist:
they exist in nature's
gravitationally pulled and precessionally elevated tidal waters of earth;
in sun-generated winds; in solar power converters;
in the chemical processes that produce methane, hydrogen, alcohol, etc.;
in thermal steam generated from the natural subterranean sources around
our planet; and in the power to be derived from temperature differential,
since heat flows spontaneously from a hot region to a cold.

There's great concern about water shortages.
The Pacific Ocean out there is very deep.
There are places where it's five miles deep,
but the average depth is one mile.

The total surface area of the earth is about 200 million square miles.
Three-quarters is water—about 150 million cubic miles of water.
That may seem like a lot of water to you and me.
The earth is 8,000 miles in diameter,
and remembering that the average ocean depth is one mile,
and one mile is 1/8,000th,
let's take this 48-inch steel ball.
Try to imagine 1/8,000. If you breathe on the steel ball, the mist from your
breath is deeper than 1/8,000th.

This tiny little film is the oceans. And we realize how incredibly small they are.

Now, besides conservation, my principal thought about water is desalinization. Using the sun to evaporate all the water we need. That's what the rain in our sky is. There's nothing new about it. We have the whole Pacific Ocean here along California, and there's a water shortage!

We've been desalinating since we had steamers. You couldn't have an ocean-going steamship without desalinization, you can't have salt in your boilers.

The man who's doing long-distance thinking says, "Well, this desalinization equipment, it'll take ten years to get it going so it'll really mean something here. What's that going to cost us? Say, 2 billion dollars." Then the mayor or the governor says, "We'd like to do some of these long-term projects, but they mean higher taxes. The people won't reelect me if I put out $2 billion for something that's going to happen ten years from now. I'm going to leave that to the next governor."

When you come to the economists, they say, "Well, it costs four cents more a thousand gallons to desalinate than to put pipes up here in the mountains."

But that's the wrong way to look at it. We have a cosmic accounting, and it's a long-distance one: What is it going to cost you *when you don't have the water?* So everyone must push, push, push for the long-distance design revolution.

This is what the World Game is about—a design revolution. How can we use principles and mind to really get things going?

I want you to really feel this with me.

The earth is revolving to obscure the sun.
The sun is not going down.
I want you to really feel this with me.
We're rolling around to obscure the sun.
We're about to have a sunclipse: the earth is revolving around very rapidly
to obscure the sun.
It's perfectly easy to feel that,
particularly if you face north and look over your left shoulder.
Just watch! and you suddenly begin to feel
this enormous earth revolving on its axis.

Incredible speed. And it's beautiful quiet motion.
And we're rolling, we're rolling around here.
You have to have your feet quite wide apart, facing to the north
and just getting the sun in the corner of your eye.
Then you feel this enormous earth revolving
here on the polar axis.

I want all of you to look at it with me now.
Look at that thing and feel this great horizon.
The sun is not doing a thing,
we are really rolling you see.
This is absolute reality.
Boy, she's really moving quite rapidly now, you really feel it.
The wider apart your legs, the more you feel it.
Now we're really going around. Boy! it's wonderful to really feel this
enormous big sphere we're on.
I've traveled around enough so I really feel it very powerfully.